A GOLFING GENIUS!

To Peter,

    I hope you will not be too
shocked to learn of the tricks some golfers
(not me!) get up to to win.

      all the best,   John

John Atkinson

Produced by *Alfresco Books*

'Mill Race', Scalegill, Kirkby Malham, Skipton, BD23 4BN

Telephone: 01729 830868

Email: jen@alfrescobooks.co.uk

ISBN: 978 1 873727 25 9

Cover   - Gordon Firth

Artwork - Gordon Firth

Pre-press - Jen Darling (*Alfresco Books*)

Printer - Ellesmere Press Ltd

To Di

ACKNOWLEDGMENTS

I would like to thank Phil Dore without whose help this book would not have been published, Jen Darling of *Alfresco Books* for her professionalism and patience, Gordon Firth for his artistry and advice, and my wife Di for being the ideal golfer's companion!

CONTENTS

Page

TEAM EFFORT

Ramsden's desert swan-song

Most sports are competitive, golf certainly is. There is only one winner. The rest, who may have practised harder, are immediately forgotten. Winning is everything. In every sport there are numerous examples of the extraordinary lengths to which sportsmen will go to attain their goals and the question must often be asked, "Is it worth it? Does the end justify the means?" That is something which each competitor must decide for himself.

There is a story concerning the journalist and golfer Leonard Crawley whose brother was even more determined than he was. As youngsters they used to go fishing and dream of catching a huge pike which would look up at them disdainfully from the safety of a deep pool. Leonard's brother swore he would get it. He did. When asked what bait his brother had used Leonard told a journalist, "None! He shot it." Unsporting you may well mutter with a sharp intake of breath and most would agree with you. Is this really playing the game? Success gained this way surely cannot provide much satisfaction.

But when Ramsden Baxter won the Old Wickian's Golf Trophy it afforded him tremendous satisfaction and his friend Willie Bradley too, for Willie had worked very hard to achieve Ramsden's victory. There were many who did not at first believe it when they were told that Ramsden had beaten Malcolm Hodge in the final. They were sure it could not happen; yet it did. Some of those who watched claimed that Ramsden had had all the luck and mentioned the unusual behaviour of the Jack Russell terrier that peed on several greens to the horror of Ramsden's opponent, the greens' chairman. They recalled with pleasure the arrival of the stunning Australian girl. And finally they agreed, after much argument, that there was nothing in the rules to prevent Ramsden using his sand wedge on the greens instead of a putter if he wished to do so, although this represented an act of great courage in view of Malcolm's temper.

Of course there was no luck involved. Nothing happened by chance. It was all planned. Ramsden's victory was one of Willie's greatest triumphs and demonstrated, as never before, his imagination, his skill at using every weapon at his disposal and his ruthlessness in striking unerringly at the soft underbelly of his opponent. "Find the Achilles Heel!" is the battle cry of every seasoned golf gamesman. With total justification it could be claimed that Willie Bradley found not only the heel but the whole leg as well. And the beauty of it was that it was all perfectly legal – questionable perhaps, but legal. Well, almost.

Most of the members were delighted when Ramsden won. Although Malcolm was greens' chairman and worked tremendously hard for the club, he was not popular. He was successful and handsome – a difficult combination. He was also a low handicap tiger. Ramsden, on the other hand, had nothing going for him. He was elderly. He never looked smart. He possessed a dishevelled sandiness entirely in keeping with his wartime occupation of tank commander in the Western Desert. And he was a dreadful golfer, especially as far as putting was concerned. In fact the rest of his game wasn't so bad and on a good day could be classed as almost mediocre, but putting always let him down. Getting the little ball into the little hole in two putts or fewer was, for him, a nightmare. But he was generous and kind-hearted and, when he lost, as he usually did, he always paid up with a smile and bought his round of drinks at the bar without complaining. He was one of the most popular members in the club and one of Willie's closest friends. And that was the nub of it, with Willie on your side only a fool would back the opposition.

In truth Malcolm wasn't really a bad chap. Circumstances had conspired against him. He had joined one of the well-known banks at an early age and his organizational skills and efficiency had resulted in rapid promotion. Now he had his own branch. He was the manager. He'd only been a member of the golf club for a few years when it was suggested he'd make a good greens' chairman. (Somebody has to do the job and there are few rewards.) To start with Malcolm enjoyed the challenge of keeping the members happy. Undoubtedly it is a challenge for there is no chance of pleasing everyone. Greens have to be hollow-tined. Greens have to be dressed. Greens have to be re-laid. The ladies are convinced that much of this work is planned for Mondays in order to scupper their Tuesday competitions. The men require perfect greens every day of the year. The head greenkeeper likes to close the course when it is flooded but many members consider it playable if only small patches of dry land are visible. Being greens' chairman is a job requiring wisdom, diplomacy and the patience of a saint. It should only be taken on for a short period otherwise the holder of the office becomes harassed, furtive, introspective and, worst of all, convinced that he and he alone knows best on all matters appertaining to the course. That was the trouble with Malcolm. He should by now have passed on his duties to somebody else. He'd been chairman for five years and had delusions of grandeur. In his opinion no-one else was capable of being greens' chairman. Now that his wife had finally left him he spent all his spare time at the club, either playing, attending meetings or simply walking the course inspecting tees, greens and fairways. When Malcolm hove into sight the head greenkeeper would jump onto the nearest tractor and drive rapidly away. Malcolm had taken to carrying binoculars with him so that he could watch players from afar and report them to the committee if they transgressed in any way – failing to smooth over bunkers or replace divots, that sort of thing. The discerning reader will by now have grasped why Malcolm had few friends.

It has to be said, however, that the three new greens laid last Autumn, at the fourth, seventh and 12th holes, were superb. This was very largely due to Malcolm's efforts. He had spent hours with the head greenkeeper designing the new greens and discussing in minute detail every aspect, from the herring-bone drainage to the type of turf. And the results were magnificent; the putting surfaces were true and the new bunkers made the holes far more interesting. Malcolm was very proud of his new greens. He liked to walk out onto the course on Sunday evenings when it was quiet and stand in front of each green. A feeling of deep contentment would seep over him for he knew deep down that he had done well, that whatever else happened those greens would always remind members of his skill and dedication. At those moments he was at peace, fulfilled and as happy as it was in his nature to be.

Ramsden Baxter had been a member longer than he cared to remember. There'd been Baxters at the Black Hills since the club was formed over a hundred years ago, and Ramsden, his father and grandfather had all been captains and presidents of the club. He'd been surprised and very upset when the greens' chairman had shouted at him one day, enquiring whether he could read, then asking why he wasn't obeying the instructions telling him to take the long steep path to the ninth tee from the eighth green rather than the much easier shorter route everybody had used for years. He thought Malcolm had been very rude. In his opinion members of a gentleman's club simply did not shout at one another on the course whatever the provocation. Malcolm had even threatened to report him to the committee. Report him to the committee indeed, who did that young whipper-snapper think he was, behaving like a little Hitler! He'd only been a member for a few years. There'd been Baxters on the committee before he was born. Why on earth were they always changing things? He'd used that old path to the ninth tee for as long as he could remember. What did it matter if it was getting worn? He wasn't going to climb that bloody hill, he'd have a thrombosis! Pity there weren't more gentlemen on the committee. That was the trouble with the club now, they let anybody in.

Such disputes, of course, are commonplace in golf clubs and are usually resolved by tact and diplomacy on the president's part and, not uncommonly, by the turning of a blind eye in certain special cases involving old and respected members. But Malcolm had been particularly obstinate on this issue and, although the president naturally supported his greens' chairman, he'd rather hoped Malcolm would let things go in Baxter's case and allow the old boy to use the easy route to the ninth tee. Not so, feathers had been ruffled, pride hurt. As the president said to his wife, the extraordinary thing was that both Ramsden and Malcolm had gone to the same boarding school and you would think they'd have been taught how to behave like adults rather than children.

And now, by a curious twist of fate, both had reached the final of the Old Wickian's Trophy and there was no question but that blood would be spilt – figuratively speaking. Malcolm would win of course for he was an excellent five handicap golfer and had won every match so far with ease. Ramsden, on the other hand, was a very shaky 25. It was extraordinary that Ramsden had got to the final at all but, owing to a suspiciously favourable draw, he hadn't encountered any golfers of ability before Malcolm. However, now he'd met his Waterloo. He'd be thrashed. Everyone knew he'd got the putting yips. He'd be lucky to win any holes. It would be a rout! The president couldn't help feeling sorry for Ramsden, whom he liked, then felt guilty about it for, undeniably, Malcolm was a key member of his committee.

A couple of weeks before the final Willie called to see Ramsden to finalise the arrangements for a short golfing holiday they were to have together in Scotland. He parked his car in the drive and gazed at the large lawn, the rockery and bushes beyond. It was a beautiful lawn, flat, green and free from weeds, almost as good as the greens at the club, apart, that was, from the unsightly brown patches which completely spoiled its appearance.

"It's Sally," explained Ramsden, coming out of the house accompanied by a small black-and-white terrier which jumped up and down excitedly barking a welcome. "Quiet, you daft dog!"

"Didn't know you had a dog Ramsden," said Willie.

"She's not mine," said Ramsden. "She belongs to my sister Janet. Do you remember Janet, Willie? She's a lot younger than I am and moved to Scotland years ago. Sadly her husband died and now she lives in Pitlochry. Her daughter Liz married an Australian and Janet's been out there for three months so we've been looking after Sally. She's due back tomorrow and Liz's coming home with her for a short holiday. I'm looking forward to seeing her again. It must be ten years since she emigrated and she was a most attractive girl. She's bringing her son Danny with her. I've never met him but hear he's a nice lad. He must be nearly eight now."

They went inside and sat in the conservatory overlooking the lawn. Ramsden's wife Connie brought tea and buttered crumpets, and the three of them reminisced nostalgically about their families. It was a glorious day and the bright sunshine made the brown patches on the lawn look even more prominent.

"She's ruined the lawn," said Ramsden, "but I'll miss the little bugger when she goes. She comes to the Gamekeeper's Arms with me every evening. Very popular there, she is. She likes Tetley's Bitter. Laps it up. The only problem is that it goes straight through her and I have to take her out every ten minutes for a pee. At closing time she helps me finish off the last pint then, when we get home, she pees again on the lawn and you can see what that's done."

He shook his head sadly but wasn't really cross for he bent down and patted Sally who rolled over obligingly, presenting her tummy for further tickling. After more attention Ramsden opened the garden door and shooed her out. She then trotted up the garden and started digging in the flower bed.

"I'll be sorry when she goes back to Scotland," admitted Ramsden. "She's really taken to me. If I've been golfing, when I come home I have to wait on the lawn whilst Connie lets her out of the house. She's always so excited to see me she pees all over the place. It's spoilt the lawn but at least it's not ruined the carpet."

Sally had now dug a large hole and unearthed a disgusting-looking bone which she was licking clean with great enjoyment.

"Wonderful nose," said Ramsden, "especially for meat. She can smell a bone if it's six inches underground."

At the time Willie had reflected on the complete dottiness of dog lovers and it was only afterwards, when he was thinking deeply about Ramsden's problem, that he remembered the conversation and realised what a valuable ally Sally could be. Ramsden's problem was the Old Boys' final. He wanted to win – desperately. In his heart of hearts he knew that never again would he get so far. If only he could make a supreme effort and win the trophy, it would be marvellous. That would be it. If he could just win this once he wouldn't care about anything else. And to beat that pompous pillock, that bossy arrogant idiot Hodge, that would really be something! But how could he do it. There'd be a slight chance if he could putt, but now that he'd got the yips he never knew where the ball would go when he hit it with his putter. If only he could use his sand wedge on the greens he'd be all right. Then he could always get down in two.

Willie listened with great interest (as he always did) when Ramsden explained for the umpteenth time why he was so good with the sand wedge. Ramsden had been with the British Eighth Army in North Africa during World War II. He'd been in charge of a tank. Even in those days he was a keen golfer and travelled everywhere with his bag of clubs. But space is limited in a Sherman tank and, with great reluctance, Ramsden had found it necessary to leave out his woods and take only a skeleton set of clubs consisting of his five and eight irons, a sand wedge and putter. Fortunately golf-balls could be popped into all sorts of nooks and crannies in a tank although they did tend to roll around. During lulls in the fighting Ramsden would take the opportunity to practise and he became particularly expert with his sand wedge. He used it the most because the balls didn't go very far and there was little chance of losing them. Ever aware of the possibility of buried mines he perfected a technique of hitting balls cleanly off the top of the sand, hardly touching the surface. This was much easier in 1942 because sand wedges had much thinner soles.

Ramsden became so good with his wedge that he used to entertain his fellow soldiers by playing a series of shots with the balls resting on top of a matchbox. He would start with short chips. then go on to full shots and the trick was never to move the matchbox. Backing himself, he won quite a lot of money and became a celebrity when it was found that certain mines could be detonated by the impact of a falling golf-ball.

After that it was a common sight to see Ramsden walking across the desert playing shot after shot with his sand wedge followed by a line of tanks keeping close to his route. Very few people knew that a consignment of golf-balls dispatched from London to General Montgomery's headquarters at Alam Haifa in 1942 were quickly sent by special messenger to Ramsden's battalion in the desert. Monty reckoned that the Allies' advance across the desert had been much quicker because of Ramsden and recommended him for a special commendation.

Willie listened in admiration to the story as he had so many times before and reflected, as he always did, on the ingenuity of the British soldier. Afterwards, when they had agreed on dates for their September weekend in Scotland, he took his leave, promising faithfully to return in a week's time to meet the travellers from Australia.

That night he slept little. Half asleep he had visions of Ramsden in North Africa with his wedge and, somehow, there was always a little dog involved, digging holes in the desert and finding all sorts of strange and sometimes unpleasant objects. Suddenly he sat up in bed, then went downstairs to make a cup of tea. Yet when he awoke in the morning he felt rested and unusually cheerful and, when he did a quick mental recap to find out why, did not at first realise what it was all about. And then it came to him. Subconsciously he'd worked out a plan, a plan that would help Ramsden in his final. It may not be enough to ensure victory but it would certainly tip the balance more in Ramsden's favour and give his old friend a far better chance of winning. It would require teamwork of the highest order however. Could the Australians play their part? Would Sally obey orders? There were so many imponderables! He'd be able to judge better next week when he'd met them. It would all depend on Danny and Liz – and Sally of course.

Ramsden's niece was even more beautiful than Willie had expected. She had long blonde hair, blue eyes and a perfectly tanned complexion. When she smiled her eyes twinkled and her whole face lit up. It was impossible not to smile with her. She spoke softly and seductively, with a slight huskiness that was both suggestive and appealing, and caused Willie Bradley to think of things long since forgotten. He had great difficulty in tearing his gaze away from those lips and eyes to inspect the rest of her. This was just as good. She had the slim graceful figure that top models yearn for. Malcolm would find her irresistible. Willy was sure of it.

Danny was playing with Sally, the little black-and-white terrier bringing back a ball that Danny threw up the garden. She wasn't very obedient however and wouldn't always return to Danny when he whistled. Obedience was crucial for the success of Willie's plan and he was becoming rather worried until Ramsden suggested straightforward bribery.

"If she returns when you whistle," Ramsden told Danny, "give her a drink of Tetley's Bitter. She'll soon learn."

She did. There were no further obedience problems but it was clear that the lawn would have many more brown patches.

When Willie explained his idea Ramsden burst out laughing. The possibility of nobbling Malcolm delighted him. Danny too was very enthusiastic and could see no difficulty in carrying out his part of the plan. He and Sally would start training immediately. Liz was happy to do anything she could. She was very fond of her uncle and delighted to have the opportunity of helping him. She thought she had some suitable clothes that might catch Malcolm's eye.

And so it was that, on the evening before the final, Ramsden, Danny and Willie set off in the gathering dusk for the golf club armed with powerful torches, a spade and two chump chops in a carrier bag. They returned over two hours later, tired and sandy, but happy in the knowledge that the first stage of their plan had been completed successfully. And Sally was impatient to be off to the Gamekeeper's Arms.

The next day was hot and sunny. The final was due to start at two o'clock. At 1.30 Connie ran Liz, Danny and Sally down to the club but, instead of stopping in the normal car park, she drove down the lane which runs past the course until she reached a secluded spot from which they could make their way unseen to their appointed places. Then she drove home to collect

Ramsden who was practising his wedge shots on the lawn. Clearly his old skills were still with him for he was chipping with great accuracy, hardly touching the turf at all.

Willie was already waiting at the club, drinking a glass of port and discussing the forthcoming match with a group of Old Wickians who had turned up to watch.

"Poor old Ramsden," said the Old Boys' secretary, Tom Hughes. "He hasn't got a chance, not against Malcolm. You can say what you like about Malcolm but he is a good golfer. You can't deny that. He'll wipe the floor with Ramsden, he will."

"I wouldn't be too sure of that if I were you," replied Willie. "I've known Ramsden a long time and I've never seen him more determined. He might surprise you. He's a real fighter when he's in the mood."

"That's all very well," said Tom, "but unfortunately he's a bloody awful putter. You know he is. It's a great shame. I wish he could beat that pompous prig but I can't see it happening. I'll tell you what, I'll bet you a fiver it's all over before the 16th. We'll all be walking in before then I'm afraid."

"Done!" said Willie. "I'll go and help Ramsden put his bag on his trolley." And so saying he went off in search of his friend.

Ramsden was putting his shoes on in the men's locker room. Even though it was a warm day he was dressed, as always, in baggy plus fours and a thick floppy pullover that couldn't quite conceal his large tummy. On his head was a large flat cap worn back to front. The idea was that the neb would stop the rain running down the back of his neck. He always wore it that way even in the middle of Summer when it wasn't raining. Ramsden produced a hip flask and they each had a swig of single malt.

"Lovely," said Willie appreciatively.

"Everything ready?" enquired Ramsden rather anxiously.

"Quite ready," replied Willie. "Don't worry about a thing."

When they got to the first tee there was no sign of Malcolm although a group of about 20 members were waiting to watch the match. The president himself was there and, after looking round rather furtively to check that Malcolm wasn't within earshot, he shook Ramsden warmly by the hand.

"Good luck," he said. "All the best. I hope you win."

"Thank you Norman," said Ramsden, much touched. "I intend to. Where's that bugger got to?"

"He's on the practice ground," replied the president. "He's been there for at least half-an-hour hitting ball after ball into the net. I'm afraid he looks to be on top form."

"Well," said Ramsden, "we'll just have to see what happens, won't we? You can never tell with this game."

And with those prophetic words he went to the putting green and tried to practise a smooth unhurried putting stroke. It was quite impossible. After a very short time Willie asked him to stop as there was no point in practising the yips and it was very unnerving for those watching to see the putter head jerking backwards and forwards convulsively.

Malcolm arrived on the tee immaculately attired in grey and black apart from his yellow cap. Willie whispered to Ramsden that he thought Malcolm looked like a carrion crow. The finalists shook hands without speaking and the president felt he ought to say something.

"Well, have a good game then," he offered rather lamely. "I hope the best man wins."

"Thank you," said Malcolm, teeing up his ball, "I will."

"Excuse me," said Ramsden, "I believe it's my honour."

"I'm five handicap, you're 25," replied Malcolm. "It's my honour."

"I don't think so," said Ramsden. "If you look at the sheet with the draw on it you'll see that my name appears first and, if you look at the rules, you'll see that Rule 10 states that the first named player on the sheet has the honour, irrespective of handicap. I'm surprised you didn't know that, a golfer of your standard. I like to stick to the rules, not like you youngsters nowadays. We used to make all new members of the club read the *Rules of Golf* before being admitted. Clearly we don't any longer."

"I'm not a new member," spluttered Malcolm. "I've been a member for 15 years!"

"Quite," said Ramsden, "a new member and one who clearly does not know the rules, more's the pity."

He bent down, removed Malcolm's ball, teed up his own and hit what was, for him, a good drive which cleared the rhododendrons and finished in the middle of the first fairway.

"Nice one Ramsden," muttered Willie. "You're getting to him already." Indeed Malcolm was exceedingly irritated at being shown to be in the wrong by an old fool like Ramsden Baxter. He gripped his driver far too tightly and swung back too quickly. The result was a high slice which finished in the bunker to the right of the fairway. He scowled and marched off the tee.

Ramsden was receiving 15 strokes from Malcolm, at that time the stroke allowance being three-quarters of the difference in handicaps. This meant that he had strokes at all but three holes, the seventh, 13th and 17th, all par threes. Both players were on the first green in three, nett two for Ramsden. The plan was that he should try his putter initially, just in case a miracle happened and he putted well. It didn't. The first putt was quite reasonable, the ball finishing a mere three feet from the hole, but then Ramsden seemed to lose control of his putter and his next putt was well wide of it. However he managed to hole his sixth for a half.

They both hit good drives at the second with Malcolm well in front of Ramsden. Ramsden had no chance of reaching the green in two and, on Willie's instructions, played a six iron down the left-hand side of the fairway, well away from the out-of-bounds on the right. As they walked towards Malcolm's long drive a girl appeared on the public footpath crossing the course in front of the green. She was ambling slowly across the fairway unaware that Malcolm was waiting to play his second shot.

"Fore!" he shouted loudly, impatiently waving his arms to hurry her across. It certainly did the trick for she looked round, startled, and hurried down the path. Indeed so great was her haste that she stumbled and fell, and the spectators heard a small cry of pain before she bravely struggled to her feet and hurried to the side of the fairway.

"Really Malcolm," called out Tom Hughes, "you're an impatient bugger! That poor girl'll have a nasty bruise."

In fact Malcolm had regretted shouting as soon as he'd opened his mouth for he saw that the person in question wasn't so much a girl as a vision of beauty whose long brown legs emerged from very short shorts and whose long blonde hair reached down to bare tanned shoulders. His mind could not have been on his game for he hit an awful second shot that finished short of the green in very rough grass half-way down a bank. Giving it hardly a glance he hurried off down the fairway calling out,

"Excuse me, I hope you're not hurt." The vision turned round in surprise and waited for him to reach her.

"I'm so sorry," said Malcolm, "I didn't mean to startle you. I do hope you haven't given yourself a nasty bump."

The girl gazed rather solemnly at Malcolm for a moment and he was struck by the blueness of her eyes and her long blonde eyelashes. Then she smiled and he saw perfect white teeth and heard her soft musical laugh.

"I think I'll survive," she said. "It was my fault. I got in your way."

"No, no!" said Malcolm, "you are quite entitled to walk across the course. It is a public right-of-way. I'm afraid I was being very impatient."

"Well there's no real harm done," said The Beautiful One, rubbing her thigh suggestively. "I don't think I'm even grazed. Can you see any scratches?" she enquired innocently of Malcolm.

"Er ... no, I can't see any scratches," said Malcolm, bending down for a better look.

"That's all right then," said the girl. "I just wanted to see the golf course but I don't want to upset anybody. I'd better go back the way I've come."

"If you'd like to see more of the course you're very welcome to walk with me," Malcolm said, rather quickly. "I'm playing in the final of a competition but, to be honest, I don't expect the match will last very long; my opponent's not very good."

The girl gave a little splutter and Malcolm thought he saw, for one brief moment, a distinctly unfriendly look in her eyes. But he must have been mistaken for then she smiled again and said softly,

"That would be most interesting. Thank you very much. I'll try not to be a nuisance."

"You won't be," said Malcolm, unaware that that was her very intention. He climbed down the bank near the green to find his ball stuck in the middle of a gorse bush. Without further ado he picked it up, conceding the hole, and hurried back to show the girl the way to the third tee.

It was of course inevitable that Malcolm would come in for a great deal of teasing about his newly acquired, and very attractive, companion. But as she was so deliciously, so exceedingly, attractive the unanimous view was that her presence was quite acceptable and that she would in no way interfere with the serious business of the final. Introductions were made all round and it transpired that she was from Australia and her name was Liz. When she offered to pull Malcolm's trolley there was even a little burst of clapping as that gentleman accepted graciously, going so far as to put his arm around her shoulder and state that he was glad to have her on his team. He won the short third in majestic style hitting a four iron to within three feet of the pin, then holing for a winning two.

Both finalists played the fourth hole well and were on the green in the same number of strokes nett, with Ramsden's ball lying quite close to the hole. As they approached the green Malcolm told Liz of all the hard work that had gone into the construction of this new green and lovingly drew her attention to the quality of the turf. He went on at some length and warmed to her even more as she asked sensibly about the importance of good drainage and was clearly interested in the construction of the green. Ramsden was walking towards his ball when a small black-and-white dog emerged from some bushes and bounded towards Ramsden barking noisily and wagging her tail. Ramsden bent down and tickled the dog under its chin whereupon it squatted down in delight and a large and rapidly growing puddle appeared from its rear end.

"Well she's pleased to see me, isn't she?" said Ramsden. "Where have you come from old girl? What's your name?"

"Is that your dog Ramsden?" asked Malcolm furiously, "because the bloody animal's ruining the green peeing on it like that. It'll kill off the grass. There'll be a big brown patch there now."

"Not my dog," replied Ramsden truthfully, "but she's a friendly little thing isn't she?" And he patted her again, producing a fresh flood.

"Don't do that!" yelled Malcolm, hurrying towards the dog waving his putter threateningly. It backed away reluctantly.

"Shoo, shoo!" shouted Malcolm. "Go away you stupid animal." He was chasing the dog off the green when suddenly there was a whistle and the little animal ran off into the woods alongside the fifth hole.

"Bloody dog!" said Malcolm, angrily. "Just look at that wet patch. I'll see if I can get one of the greens' staff to hose it down." And he hurried off to the nearest green-keeper who was raking a bunker about 200 yards away, shouting and waving as he ran. When he returned he was hot and very cross, so it was not surprising that he took three putts whilst Ramsden managed to get down in two to win the hole.

The fifth is a long par five. The green is not visible from the tee as the fairway initially ascends before turning left slightly, then sloping gently down to the green. Malcolm had cooled down by now, helped by the sympathy and understanding of his beautiful caddie, and he hit two majestic woods close to the green. Ramsden, on the other hand, hit a succession of appalling shots and, after playing five, was still short of a drainage ditch running across the fairway 150 yards from the green. Even if he reached the green in two more he would be lucky to hole out in nine and was sure to lose the hole. As they approached the ditch however the green came into view and everyone stopped in amazement, for the little black-and-white dog was digging furiously in the bunker by the green, spraying sand and soil all over the flawless turf.

"I don't believe it!" shouted Malcolm. "It's that bloody dog again. It's digging a bloody pit. Why's it digging there?" he enquired of nobody in particular.

"Well don't just stand there gawping Malcolm," said the president. "You're the greens' chairman. You'd better go and chase it off before it does any more damage."

Willie looked at Ramsden. Ramsden smiled at Willie. What a stroke of luck that the president should say that. They couldn't have planned it better!

So Malcolm set off again, running as fast as he could towards the green. But he was too late to stop the little animal from pulling a large meaty chop out of the bunker then rapidly making off with it into the woods. When Malcolm reached the bunker he saw a large hole where the dog had been digging. He used the bunker rake and carefully filled in the hole, smoothing over the sand. Perfect. Then, hot and harassed, he walked slowly back up the fairway.

"Well done Malcolm," said the president.

"My hole I believe," said Ramsden.

"Pardon!" said Malcolm in amazement.

"Commendable though your action was in raking that bunker and filling in the hole, I'm afraid it constitutes a breach of Rule 13.2. You've improved your line of play because you have to go over the bunker to get on the green. The penalty in Match Play is that you lose the hole. Sorry, but I think we should play according to the rules. I like to do things properly. You may think I'm old-fashioned but I do believe that standards must be maintained."

Well of course there was much discussion among the onlookers and rule books were produced and studied, but Ramsden was quite correct and they moved on to the next hole with Ramsden now two up.

"We didn't plan that," said Willie, looking hard at Ramsden. "We just expected Sally's digging to upset him. How did you know about that rule?"

"I read it up last night – thought it might be useful," whispered Ramsden.

"It certainly was," said Willie, gazing at his friend in admiration. "You're

a cunning old bugger!"

"If I see that bloody dog again I'll kill it," muttered Malcolm to Liz as they walked to the sixth tee.

The sixth hole was played in stony silence. Malcolm won it easily because Ramsden took four putts. Willie decided that the time had come for his friend to stop using the putter.

The seventh is a picturesque little hole with a beck flowing behind the green. Malcolm reached the green with a good iron shot but was unfortunate in getting too much run, the ball finally finishing well past the hole. Ramsden hit a dreadful shot, topping the ball badly, but it ran all the way down the slope, just missed the bunker on the right and finished on the green. He was also a long way from the pin although slightly nearer than Malcolm.

As they walked towards the green Willie complimented Malcolm on the state of the green. In his opinion, of the three new greens this was the best as it rewarded the player brave enough to attack the hole from the tee. Malcolm had designed the green on two layers. The flag was on the top layer but both balls were on the bottom layer, beyond which there was a little bank and then the stream. Those players whose balls finished on the top plateau had much easier putts. From the lower level, where both Malcolm and Ramsden were, it required a great deal of skill to get close to the hole. Malcolm felt confident that he could do this and was certain that Ramsden couldn't. He didn't have to give Ramsden a stroke, so after this hole the match should be all square.

When everyone stopped by the side of the green Malcolm was surprised to see Willie handing Ramsden a heavy sand wedge. Ramsden walked to the rough grass beyond the green and had several practice swings, removing large lumps of turf each time. Then he walked back to the green and addressed his ball – with the sand wedge!

"Hey!" shouted out Malcolm. "What are you doing? You can't use that wedge on the green."

"Why not?" asked Ramsden. "There's nothing in the rules to stop me."

"But you'll damage the green," said Malcolm. "You must use a putter."

"I don't have to use a putter," replied Ramsden. "I can putt with whatever club I like. Ben Crenshaw did in that Ryder Cup match in America."

"But you'll spoil the green," stuttered Malcolm, looking down at the immaculate surface. "You'll take out a divot. You'll ruin the green!"

"I'll try not to," replied Ramsden. "Don't worry. It's you to putt first anyway."

Malcolm was understandably upset. He looked towards the president for support but, although that worthy gentleman was shaking his head in amazement, he motioned to Malcolm to carry on, indicating that nothing could be done. Malcolm putted. His ball failed to get up the slope to the top plateau and rolled backwards. It was a weak, poor putt, but what could you expect? Malcolm wasn't concentrating on the putt at all, he was thinking about Ramsden. He felt very agitated. He covered his face with his hands as Ramsden lined up his wedge shot and therefore didn't see the beautiful little chip shot that Ramsden played, dropping the ball gently beside the hole. But he heard the applause and, when he looked at the surface of the green, could detect no mark.

"Just lucky that time," called out Ramsden cheerfully. "Managed to take it cleanly."

Malcolm now had to hole a horrible eight foot putt up the slope with a left to right borrow to halve the hole. He missed it – two down once again.

At that stage Willie could be forgiven for feeling a little smug. Everything was going so well. All his plans were working. His old friend was two in front. He smiled. He should have known better! It is at times like this, when the golfer is lulled into a false sense of security, that fate steps in to show who's the real boss. It wasn't that Ramsden stopped trying, not at all, just the opposite in fact, he tried too hard and his golf over the next four holes was dreadful. He topped. He shanked. He sliced. He hooked. There seemed to be no end to the variety of bad shots he was capable of playing. On the 12th tee his swing was so wild he almost missed the ball completely. It toppled off the tee peg and just made it into the ditch in front of the tee. He had completely lost his grip on the match. He was two down, very probably soon to be three.

"My God, Willie, I can't do a bloody thing," he muttered in despair as the two walked together to the ditch.

"Ramsden," said Willie, "it's at times like this that we old campaigners really show our mettle. Remember it's the12th and Sally's waiting by the green. And just look at that cocky young upstart showing off to young Liz. Remember you're a Baxter and a Baxter must never be beaten by a Hodge!"

"That's all very well Willie," replied Ramsden, "but I can't hit a bloody shot right! I've no idea how to swing."

"You are going to relax," said Willie sternly. "Think of one shot at a time and play your wedge only, like you did in the Western Desert. You'll soon get your confidence back."

And so Ramsden took several deep breaths, dropped out of the ditch under penalty of one stroke, then played two good wedge shots. He was four nett three when they reached Malcolm's drive. Malcolm judged it was about 160 yards to the pin. He selected a six iron and prepared to play his shot. At this moment the little black and white terrier appeared from a small copse of trees and ran across the green to the new bunker on the right-hand side. Malcolm stopped in amazement. After sniffing around for a very short time the dog began to dig in the soft sand, throwing a shower of it in all directions.

"It's that Jack Russell again," said the president. "I don't know what you put in those new bunkers of yours, Malcolm, but there must be something very tasty in there."

"There's only sand and hard core for drainage," said Malcolm. "There's nothing else."

"Well that little bugger's found a nice bone," observed the president as Sally carried something onto the green and sat down to lick it enthusiastically.

"Clear off!" yelled Malcolm. "Shoo! Shoo!"

However the little dog took no notice and Malcolm had to run almost to the green before it picked up the bone and ambled off towards the trees. Willie, who was watching closely, experienced a twinge of anxiety, for he saw Sally moving unsteadily as she followed a zigzag path across the green. She tripped up twice but never let go of the bone, then stopped for a rest at the side of the green. Then, as Malcolm started chasing her again, she stood up shakily and toppled sideways into the greenside bunker. All was well, however, because she scrambled out at her second attempt and tottered off into the trees still holding the precious bone.

"Looks to me as if Sally's had a drop too much to drink," Willie said to Ramsden. "I hope she can stay upright for a little while longer."

By now Malcolm had retraced his steps to his drive. Hot and very irritated he played his second shot far too quickly, hitting a high slice that finished in the same bunker visited by Sally a few minutes earlier.

"Hard luck Malcolm," said the president. "Anyway you'll be able to repair the damage in that bunker, but remember, not until you've played your shot."

"I know that!" snarled Malcolm crossly.

Ramsden reached the green with two more wedge shots. Malcolm was very irritated, but not particularly concerned for he would be on the green for three and Ramsden was nett five. However, when he reached the bunker he saw that his ball had a large stone resting behind it, obviously dug up by Sally. Now many golf clubs have Local Rules permitting stones to be removed from bunkers, but not ours. When it had been suggested a few years ago that players should be allowed to do this Malcolm had objected strongly, pointing out that ours is not a seaside links and there should be no stones in the bunkers at the Black Hills Golf Course not, that is to say, if the green-keepers did their jobs properly. And now here he was with a bloody boulder just behind his ball. It wasn't fair! That damned dog! He would have to lay the club face very open and hit much further behind the ball than normal. Then both ball and stone should pop out onto the green. He could do it. He'd show them!

But just as he was concentrating hard, intent on playing his shot, there was a commotion in the bushes and the small dog appeared again. Running across the green towards Ramsden, she fell over frequently and barked between hiccups with a strange 'wooshing' sound. When she reached Ramsden she squatted down happily and a huge puddle spread rapidly over the surface of the green.

"My God!" said the president enviously. "What capacity! You wouldn't think a little dog that size could do so much – and so quickly!"

"Get her off!" yelled Malcolm. "Chase her off the green." He then watched in horror as the pool disappeared into the surface of the new green. Ramsden picked up Sally, who snuggled down in his arms, fell asleep and began to snore gently.

"Come on," he said, "let's see if we can find your owner." He carried the little dog off the green and walked down the public footpath through the trees. There was a faint whistle, Sally woke up, wriggled free and disappeared into the bushes.

Malcolm was speechless. Once again he addressed his ball, but somehow he didn't see the golf-ball but instead a small black-and-white terrier. With a great release of pent-up anger he hit down viciously and ball, stone and sand flew out of the bunker. The ball was still rising as it passed over the spectators at the side of the green and clattered into the bushes beyond.

"Better play another Malcolm," advised the president. "We'll never find it in there."

"Leave the bloody thing," said Malcolm crossly. "I'm not bothering. Ramsden can have the hole."

Only one down now! Ramsden felt like a new man. He played an excellent shot at the short 13th, then chipped the ball directly into the hole for a winning two. The match was all square.

As Malcolm walked despondently towards the 14th tee Liz put her hand on his arm. He looked down in surprise and noted what a very attractive brown hand it was.

"You know," she said, "you've been very unlucky, very unlucky indeed. I think you've played wonderfully in view of everything that's happened."

"Well thank you," said Malcolm, "that's very kind of you. I think I have been unlucky. Some very strange things have happened this afternoon. I can't remember seeing a dog digging up a bunker before."

Now at this point, and in spite of family loyalties, Liz was feeling sorry for Malcolm and had almost decided not to interfere with the match over the next few holes in the manner previously arranged with Willie. Unfortunately for him, however, Malcolm didn't stop there.

"These old codgers make me sick!" he said. "They think they own the course and can do what they like. They think they can still play golf too. It makes you laugh just watching that old fool trying to swing, but I'll sort him out now, you just watch me!"

And with those few unkind words Malcolm sealed his fate and Liz knew she would play the leading role in the final part of Willie's plan.

As they walked together down the 14th hole Liz moved very close to Malcolm, so close in fact that he felt her leg brushing against his thigh and became aware of the alluring, sensuous smell of her perfume. He looked at her in surprise and saw her gazing at him in rapt admiration.

"I have enjoyed it so much this afternoon," she said in a low husky voice. "It's such a pity the match will end soon and I won't see you again."

"I ... I'll ... I'll just play my second shot," stammered Malcolm. Confused by this unexpected turn of events and conscious of all sorts of thoughts racing through his mind, he played the shot far too quickly and the ball did a quick nose-dive into the ditch short of the green.

"Damn!" said Malcolm.

"That was all my fault," said Liz, her voice sinking until it was barely more than a whisper. "I shouldn't have spoken. I shouldn't have let you know how I feel. I'm so sorry."

"Not at all," replied Malcolm. "I'm glad you did. Don't worry, that shot was all my fault, nothing to do with you. It's only a game after all."

It was when Willie heard this remark that he knew Malcolm was hooked – that *Operation Distraction* was well underway. Accordingly, he gave Ramsden the sand wedge and instructed him to play short of the ditch for three so that he could reach the green in four and then, with two more wedge shots, hole out in six nett five. It was good enough. Malcolm picked out of the ditch for three but failed to put his fourth close enough to the pin to get a five, and Ramsden won the hole.

The 15th hole is a long par five, so long in fact that Ramsden couldn't play his trusty wedge all the way. It would have taken him six wedge shots to reach the green even if they were all hit perfectly. He took a three wood from the tee and sliced his ball into the trees on the right. Malcolm hit a long straight drive.

As Liz and Malcolm walked together up the fairway Liz put her arm through Malcolm's and drew him even closer.

"I wonder," she said softly, "I wonder whether it would be all right if I took my top off. It's so hot. Would it be all right. Would you mind?"

"Err. ... well ... err ... no, I wouldn't mind," stammered Malcolm. "But I'd better just check with the president first. There are various rules about dress on the course. I'll just have a word with him."

The president was quite taken aback by this unusual request and found it necessary to consult several of the spectators. It was pointed out that men were not allowed to remove their shirts on the course, however no-one knew of any regulation preventing ladies from doing so. However, nobody had ever seen any of the lady members without a top. But there again Liz wasn't a member, she was a caddie, and there weren't any dress regulations about caddies other than that they should be decently attired. The president, noting with relief that no ladies were present, finally decided that it all depended on what Liz was wearing underneath. He therefore suggested to Malcolm that, if she did take her top off, he would be able to judge better whether she was attired decently. So she did, revealing a brief bikini top that left nothing to the imagination and caused an immediate ripple of applause, which was quickly stifled as the president looked round askance.

"Well," he said, "err .... well, errm .... fine .... fine. No problem."

And with that he walked on hurriedly, trying not to look in Liz's direction as everybody else was doing and wondering what the ladies' section would do when they heard. At the very least there'd be a letter from their committee. Oh well, he'd meet that problem when it happened.

Malcolm didn't so much win the 15th as have it thrown at him. Ramsden failed to get out of the trees with his first two attempts and finally picked his ball up in disgust when he'd taken nine and still hadn't reached the green. All square again. Willie sighed. There was only so much that he could do. Ramsden must pull himself together or all would be in vain.

On the way to the 16th tee Liz moved close to Malcolm and put her arm through his.

"You are so strong," she said, stroking his forearm. "You hit the ball so far I can't even see it land. How far can you hit it?"

"If I hit a really good one here I can get on the green," said Malcolm. "It's about 320 yards but it's a bit downhill."

"Can you really!" exclaimed Liz. "That's amazing. Ooh, I would like to see you do that. Will you try for me? Will you hit it as hard as you can?"

"Of course," said Malcolm. "Just watch this!"

He gripped the club tightly and lashed at the ball, swinging far too quickly. His shot was a big hook finishing well wide of the green. Willie smiled and relaxed slightly; all was going according to plan. Ramsden then played his reliable old wedge from the tee, then again on the fairway and finally onto the green. He was receiving a stroke and the hole was halved. On the green Willie had made great play of examining Ramsden's putt from every angle and advising him of the line to take to the hole. There were many watching who wondered why he bothered, pointing out that Ramsden hadn't used his putter since the sixth and with a wedge it didn't matter at all about the borrows as the ball didn't run along the ground anyway. But Willie knew what he was doing and, as they all walked to the 17th tee, Liz spoke up right on cue,

"I'd like to see if I could find the line to the hole for you," she told Malcolm. "I do so want to help. Could I try at this hole please?"

"Of course you can," replied Malcolm, knowing full well that whatever line she suggested he'd use his own judgment anyway. "You can tell me the line on this green."

On the 17th tee Willie looked around. There was an excited buzz of chatter from the spectators. There was so much to talk about. It had been a most entertaining match, with dogs and bones, and beautiful blondes wearing very few clothes. Willie had already won his bet with the Old Boys' secretary. Tom Hughes said he was delighted to pay up, he'd never dreamt it would be such a good match.

Willie smiled as he saw the group surrounding Malcolm. It wasn't Malcolm they were interested in, it was his caddie. Liz was so attractive, Malcolm hadn't had any chance of resisting her charms. But now there was the 17th to cope with and Ramsden was looking distinctly weary. Also, he didn't get a stroke and couldn't play his wedge from the tee because he couldn't hit it far enough to clear the rough between tee and green.

It was a critical hole. If everything went according to plan it wouldn't matter how many Ramsden took, he would win the hole anyway. But would everything go according to plan? That was the big question. If only Ramsden could play the hole well it wouldn't matter but he looked so tired. Willie sighed. He too felt exhausted.

Malcolm hit a fine shot with his six iron into the heart of the green. There was a ripple of applause. He stepped back, pleased, and smiled at Liz who smiled back with a warmth that made life seem wonderful to him. What a girl! He'd ask her out to dinner that evening to thank her for caddying. And afterwards ... well, who knew what might happen. He felt young again, alive, in command!

The hush that descended as Ramsden addressed his ball was soon followed by a groan as he shanked his three iron onto the first green. From the first green he visited the 18th fairway and the second tee before finally reaching the green in four. He chipped close to the hole for five and Malcolm magnanimously gave him a six. Why didn't Ramsden give Malcolm the hole, the gallery wondered? Malcolm would never take more than three putts. He would still win the hole if he took four putts. It was very strange.

Malcolm was pleased. He was sure to win the hole. It was just a question of going through the motions. He'd ask Liz to give him the line. She'd like that. And so, in the best traditions of all the great caddies, Liz bent down with Malcolm and looked at the line from behind the ball, and they discussed humps and hollows and little borrows in a very learned and quite unnecessary fashion. Then, as he addressed the ball, she walked to the other side of the hole and knelt down to check that the line selected was the right one. And that was Malcolm's undoing. As he gazed at her kneeling behind the hole he saw that her magnificent cleavage was directly in line with the hole and, as she leaned further and further forward, he saw that the brief bikini top had slipped and that, at any moment, much more would be revealed than his caddie intended. He heard a low whistle from the admiring audience and, without thinking, putted quickly, anxious to avoid embarrassment for her. The ball stopped by the hole and he tapped it in quickly before walking off the green.

"Malcolm!" called out Ramsden.

"Yes?" replied Malcolm.

"I'm afraid I shall have to claim that hole," said Ramsden. "Unfortunately your caddie was still kneeling behind the hole giving you the line when you putted and, of course, that is not permitted according to Rule 8-2(b). The penalty is loss of hole I believe."

"Errr ... yes, of course, you're quite right," muttered Malcolm. "I wasn't thinking."

"Well, not about golf that's for sure!" said the president. "Hard luck Malcolm, Ramsden's right, you lose the hole."

One up now and one to play. Ramsden only had to halve the last hole to win the trophy. Only a half! Surely he could manage that. But he felt exhausted, completely drained. He saw his old friend Willie looking at him worriedly and his niece Liz smiling encouragingly. How well she'd played her part! How well they'd all done, including his little friend Sally. He took a deep breath.

"Right!" he said. "Let's get on with this match." And he hit a solid five iron down the middle to loud applause.

Malcolm was bemused. He had the feeling that somehow he'd been manipulated. He couldn't understand it but he wouldn't give in without a struggle. If he could somehow win the 18th they'd have to go down the first again and play 'sudden death' until someone won a hole. And old Ramsden looked so dreadful Malcolm felt sure he wouldn't get very much further. With hope renewed Malcolm smashed a long drive nearly onto the green. He strode briskly down the fairway, sure that he could get a birdie three.

After some discussion Willie and Ramsden decided that Ramsden would have to play a wooden club for his second shot in order to try and reach the green. A four nett three would certainly halve the hole, if not win it, and give Ramsden the match and the Old Boys' trophy. Ramsden hit a good shot which, unfortunately, trickled into the bunker at the side of the green. There was a chorus of sympathetic "Oohs" and "Aahs", and many "Hard Lucks", one of which came from Malcolm. For all golfers find sympathy in their hearts when their opponents are in deep trouble.

Malcolm put his second dead. Quite dead. Indisputably dead. It was a superb shot. There was applause. He permitted himself a little smile. He was pleased. He felt sure he'd win the hole now. He'd beat the old bugger yet! He looked at Liz and was surprised to see that she looked upset. Upset! Why should she look upset? He was baffled. He couldn't understand it.

Ramsden looked at his ball lying cleanly in the bunker, perhaps 15 yards from the hole. Willie handed him the old sand wedge with the rusty shaft, the club that had served him so well in the Western Desert. Ramsden recalled those times and how he used to be able to drop a ball on a buried mine just about where the hole was. And then he didn't see the hole any more but a buried mine surrounded by sand. He had no recollection of playing the shot but heard a great roar as the ball dropped straight into the hole.

The next thing he remembered was his old friend rushing up shouting, "You've done it! You've won! You've bloody well won!" He then shook his hand so vigorously it hurt.

He was surrounded by well-wishers all congratulating him, patting him on the back, anxious to shake his hand. Even Malcolm pushed his way through the crowd and said, "Well done!" rather grudgingly before moving off to look for his caddie. And when the realization came to Ramsden that he had actually achieved his ambition, that he had actually won the Old Wickian's Golf Trophy, he felt so pleased that he shouted,

"First drink's on me!" After which there was a loud cheer and a sudden rush towards the bar.

As they left the 18th green Ramsden glanced back and caught sight of his niece. She smiled and winked at him – just once. Then, taking the hand of a small boy carrying a small dog, she disappeared into the trees.

THE CULL LIST

In which the benefits of having a caddie are illustrated.

When Dr Sean Cranleigh met the secretary in the gents' locker room and Arthur asked him to pop into the office for a little chat, old Sean was intrigued and, after changing rather more quickly than usual, hurried along to the secretary's office to see what it was all about. He thought Arthur would want his advice, perhaps on a medical matter or, more likely, on something to do with the club, for Sean was a past president and past presidents, in his view, still had a great deal to offer. Yes, that must be it, Arthur wanted a quiet word, a bit of advice. He'd maybe like to know how they'd tackled something in the past. Well Sean was his man. He'd help him sort it all out and be glad to! He tapped on the office door and went in briskly without waiting for an invitation.

But when he'd listened for over ten minutes to Arthur talking about the weather, his holidays, his wife and his rheumatism, it suddenly struck Sean that the secretary was distinctly uncomfortable and was putting off, for as long as possible, the real reason for their chat. What on earth was the matter? The two of them had been friends for years and he couldn't imagine what was troubling the little man.

"Arthur," he said, "for God's sake stop wittering and get to the point. Tell me what's on your mind."

"Aah," said the secretary. "Well all right then. You're not going to like this Sean and I must say I don't either. I think it's all so bloody silly. Why the committee spends so much time on piddling little things when they ought to be discussing important issues like decorating the clubhouse beats me."

"For heaven's sake Arthur," said Sean impatiently, "what on earth are you on about?"

"There was a committee meeting last night," said the secretary in a rush. "One of the committee made a complaint about you and I was instructed to tell you that, unless you change your ways, further action will have to be taken." He stopped for breath, waiting for the explosion.

"Me!" said Sean. "There's been a complaint about me! What on earth am Oi supposed to have done? Why would anyone complain about me? Tell me, Oi'll will be most interested to know!"

"Changing your shoes in the car park," replied the secretary. "You know you sometimes do and it's against the rules."

"Changing my shoes in the car park," repeated Sean. "Do you mean someone's actually complained about that?"

"I do," replied the secretary. "Made quite a thing about it he did. Said it lowered the whole tone of the club and you ought to know better. Pointed out that there were notices all around the clubhouse asking members to observe the rules about dress and to change in the locker rooms. It's true of course."

'Oi know it's bloody well true," spluttered Sean, "but you know as well as Oi do that my knees are troubling me a lot these days and it's two flights of stairs up from the car park to the locker rooms. Oi usually put my golf shoes on sitting in my car because it saves me climbing up all those bloody steps. Nobody notices!"

"Well, Jul ... I mean somebody has!" retorted the secretary.

"It's that bloody young upstart Julian Prince!" spluttered Sean, his face growing redder and redder. "That pompous, conceited, arrogant little prig. He's only been a member five minutes. How he ever got elected to the committee beats me! Are you telling me that that interfering busybody has had the cheek to complain about me? Me – a past president of this club! That social-climbing, self-opinionated know-all ... that ... that smug southern twit." He paused for breath and the secretary attempted to soothe his old friend.

"Calm down! Calm down!" he said, "and have a drink of this." He handed Sean a glass with a generous measure of whisky in it and poured one for himself, reflecting that every golf club secretary should keep a bottle in his desk drawer for occasions such as this when oil needs to be poured on troubled waters.

After two more whiskies and a long discussion about new members who should never have been admitted to the club, they both felt better. Sean drove home deep in thought. He still felt hurt and very annoyed. That bloody Julian! And then he remembered that he and his friend Willie Bradley were in the semi-final of the Four Ball Cup and had to play Julian Prince and his partner Mitchell Binns in the next round. Mitch was all right, but Julian – that bloody Julian! Well that match would have to be cancelled for a start! There was no way he'd ever play golf with Julian Prince again. They'd have to give them the match and make bloody sure Julian and Mitch knew why! They'd tell them they were choosy with whom they played; they only played against gentlemen! He'd have a word with Mitch and tell him it wasn't his fault. Yes, that's what he'd do. He'd have to tell Willie and then he'd write a letter to Julian. He knew just what he'd say! Come to think of it he might as well call on Willie now, it was on his way home, and put him in the picture. Willie'd understand.

Sean was one of Willie's closest friends. He it was who, each September for many years, accompanied Willie, Ramsden and Angus on their September trips to Scotland. For four glorious carefree days they would play golf at St Andrews or Gullane or Troon, or wherever. As a GP it was Sean's role to look after the health of the party and provide tablets for headaches, backaches and the variety of bowel complaints that sometimes afflict golfers when they snatch a few days away from the hustle and bustle of everyday life to indulge in battery charging with friends. And whilst it is undeniably true that Angus, a Scot, always maintained that he would have to be at death's door before he would take anything prescribed by that bloody Irishman, the fact of the matter is that when Sean insisted that the four must drink a glass of Glenmorangie followed by one of Laphraoig, then Talisker, last thing at night to preserve their good health, the Scotsman never argued and the medicine was remarkably effective for, over the years, no-one missed the 7.30am call for bacon, eggs, black pudding, tomatoes, mushrooms and fried bread.

In his days as a practising GP Sean had maintained a firm bedside manner. His reputation had soared after he'd visited a lady member with a bad bout of flu.'

"Now, ye're te stay in bed Mary and drink plenty," admonished Sean, "and ye're not to get up till Oi tell yer ye can. That husband of yours'll have to look after himself for a while – and you too. Are ye listening to me Mary? Are ye hearin' what Oi'm tellin' ye?"

"Yes doctor," replied Mary, who hadn't the strength to argue. "I'll not get up till you say I can, I promise."

"Good girrrl," said Sean. "Ye must do that."
And she did.

Unfortunately Sean forgot all about her. Some three weeks later he met her husband at the golf club and that worthy gentleman said rather diffidently,

"Oh, by the way Sean, Mary's ever so much better now. Quite recovered. And actually we've both been wondering when she can get up?"

"B'Jaysus!" exclaimed Sean, "Oi'd compl ... Oi'll call round in the morning. Your Mary needed a good rest. Very run down she was," he went on firmly, seeing a way out. "She'll be much better now, ye'll see." And of course she was. The long rest had done her a power of good. After that the ladies looked upon Sean as one of the old school of caring doctors who didn't just hand out pills but prescribed sensible remedies which went to the root of the problem. His practice grew rapidly.

Sean considered himself a pretty fine diagnostician, one of the best. He claimed he could tell what was wrong with most of his patients before they ever opened their mouths. It was all a question of observation he would say – of looking into their eyes, watching them when they walked in, that sort of thing. Probably most of the time he was right, but not always. On one occasion he was called into the 19th to examine an elderly member slumped in a corner, breathing shallowly, a nasty colour. Sean immediately rang for the emergency ambulance and dispatched the gentleman forthwith to the infirmary with a suspected coronary. The member got a nasty shock when he woke up after his heavy lunchtime drinking session and subsequent nap to find himself tucked up in hospital in intensive care wired up to all sorts of gadgets. It was a poor do if a fellow couldn't have a quiet snooze at his own golf club without being carted off without so much as a by-your-leave to the local hospital where he might catch anything, he protested indignantly on his way home. But, as Sean pointed out tight-lipped on the many occasions when the story was retold at the club, you can't take any chances, it might have been a coronary, it was just bad luck that it wasn't!

But even that episode paled into insignificance when compared with his diagnosis of the medical problems of the Gleneagles' caddie, when Sean, with all his experience, failed to spot the obvious. It all began when the four of them – for they all travelled in one car – crossed the border into Scotland. Unusually for him the Irishman had been silent for several minutes and, when he did speak, it was clear that he'd come to an important decision.

"When we play on the King's Course," he said, "Oi'm going to have a caddie – a proper caddie. Oi don't care what it costs. Oi'm going to have a caddie."

There was a stunned silence. A caddie! They never had caddies! They weren't American, or Japanese. They were British!

"You don't want a caddie," said the Scot. "It won't do you a scrap of good. You couldn't hit the ball where he told you to anyway, so what's the point? It will just be a waste of money!"

"It will not!" replied the Irishman firmly. "Oi'm playin' very well at de moment. Oi'm swingin' much more slowly."

"You, swinging slowly!" exclaimed Ramsden. "You've never swung slowly in your life. You couldn't! Your swing's just a blur it's so fast. You can't stop it with f11 at a five hundredth – I know I've tried."

"Camera shake!" said Sean. "You drink too much. Anyway Oi don't care. Oi want a caddie. Oi deserve a caddie! Oi work bloody hard all year round. Oi'm goin' to have a caddie."

"If you want a caddie you have a caddie Sean," said Willie who was driving. "You and I are playing together tomorrow at Gleneagles. We'll show these two buggers. They'll be sorry they haven't got caddies when we thrash them."

And so, in spite of the scorn and derision heaped on him by Angus and Ramsden all that day in the best traditions of good fellowship, the next morning the Irishman went to the caddiemaster and returned a few minutes later to collect his bag from the boot of the car.

"He asked me if Oi wanted a bag carrier for £12, a Class B caddie for £15 or a Class A caddie for £20 plus tip," reported Sean. "So Oi told him Oi wanted his best man at £20."

"Well!" muttered the Scotsman, "you're crackers but you GP's make so much money I suppose you've got to spend it somehow."

Before Sean could reply a very tall, very thin, very scruffy young man walked up. Long untidy hair hung down to his shoulders and he had a ring in his nose.

"It's Sean's bloody caddie!" whispered Ramsden in delight.

"Which one o' yer's Doctorrr Cranleigh?" enquired the scruffy one. "It's a fine moan for goalf." He picked up Sean's bag and walked over to the first tee.

"Oi'm not having that long-haired git," spluttered Sean. "Oi'm gettin' anudder one." He hurried back to the caddiemaster's office.

Willie, Angus and Ramsden walked down the road the front of the clubhouse and headed towards the starter's box and the first tee. They were looking forward to playing again on the King's Course and intrigued to see who would turn up this time to carry Sean's clubs. Little did they realise that the man who would shortly join the party, would have such a profound influence, both then and in the future, on Sean's golfing activities.

Jamie was a remarkable sight. He was small and broad, almost as broad as he was tall. He wore an ancient tweed jacket with wide padded shoulders over a string vest. His trousers, silver grey and very soiled, tapered down to heavy black boots. When not carrying a bag he leant to one side, for one leg was bent and shorter than the other. But his most striking feature – unforgettable and at first sight very upsetting – was his face. The left side was squashed to the right. The left eye sunken and almost closed. The nose flattened sideways. The mouth pushed round. He spoke out of the side with a thick Glasgow accent. His black hair was cropped close, little longer than the stubble on his chin. He looked frightening.

"Ma name's Jamie," he announced. "Ah'm te caddie fer t' doctorrr."
This time Sean didn't argue. He daredn't.

They all hit good drives and, as they walked down the first fairway, the other three overheard Sean talking to his caddie. He was conversing in that friendly man-to-man fashion calculated to establish a good master and caddie relationship. They smiled. It was Sean at his Irish best.

"Now Jamie," he said, "Oi'm a doctor, as ye know, and Oi can see ye've a leedle problem wid yer face. And Oi can tell ye that Oi've seen dis same problem many toimes before and Oi knows what it is. It's very common and Oi can assure ye it'll get better. It's an affliction of the nerves in the face and Oi can tell ye that it'll disappear as quickly as it came and ye'll soon be back to ye're old self again. Ye will, believe me!"

There was a long silence. Then Jamie spoke.

"It'll no' get better," he said, sadly. "Ah was hit by a bloody truck! It was the drrrink that did it. Ah was drrrunk a' the time."

After that the others always treated Sean's diagnoses with suspicion. After all a doctor who cannot distinguish between nerve problems and a simple case of truck damage must be unreliable. They were forced to admit though that, in spite of his awful appearance, Jamie was a splendid caddie. He quickly assessed Sean's capabilities and shepherded him round the famous course with great skill. Sean and Willie won five and four. Sean was delighted and hurried off to buy a bottle of whisky – Grouse of course, no other would have done. Jamie fetched five glasses and they sat overlooking the 18th green drinking contentedly, listening to Jamie telling tales of the past, of famous golfers and famous occasions.

When Sean reached my uncle's house he'd cooled down a lot but Willie knew immediately that something was wrong. He listened in silence whilst Sean told him what the secretary had said and puffed away at his old pipe for several minutes more before speaking.

"Did you hear," he enquired, "about that disgraceful episode when Julian Prince told Horace that he'd been a member far too long and should retire to enable new members to join! And then the next day Julian and three of his friends sat at Horace's table in the bar lounge and wouldn't budge when Geoff told them that Horace and the others always sat there and nobody else ever did. You can't blame Geoff of course, he's only the bar man, he couldn't stop them sitting there, but can you imagine anyone else in the club having the brass neck to sit in the seats that three past presidents have sat in for the past 40 years! When Horace and the others arrived a bit later they were very put out and Julian was quite rude to them. He told them there were plenty of other seats available. Imagine that! They didn't stay of course. They went home immediately, very upset! I believe Horace's had a word with the president but he can't do anything."

The two old friends contemplated in silence the rudeness and brashness of certain new members and agreed that these members could not be classified as gentlemen and should never have been admitted to the club.

"We'll move Julian Prince to the top of the Cull List," said Sean.

"Undoubtedly!" agreed Willie.

The Cull List had been established some years previously by Willie and his friends. It was a secret list of golfers who, in the opinion of this select group, should never have been allowed to become members of the Black Hills Golf Club and who should be encouraged to leave at the earliest possible opportunity. The group was, of course, aware that once a member has been accepted it is very difficult to get rid of him (or her) unless they leave of their own accord. However if he (or she) can be persuaded by any means – any means at all, fair or foul – to resign, then all's well and there's room for the next chap on the Waiting List. The little group took its duties very seriously, reviewing the list regularly, then scheming and plotting to try to get rid of members they considered undesirable, always with the best interests of the club at heart of course!

"What do you think then," asked Sean, "shall Oi write to that bugger telling him we've no intention of playing them?"

"No!" said Willie thoughtfully, "I don't think that's the right thing to do at all. I think we should play them and beat them, and do all we can to bring that unkind, self-opinionated upstart down a peg or two. Tell you what, we'll see if we can persuade that caddie friend of yours, Jamie, to come down from Gleneagles and spend a few days with us. You're still in touch with him aren't you? I reckon we might need his help. He could come in very useful."

His voice trailed away and a faraway look came into his eyes. The old grey cells had clicked into gear and Sean, who knew his friend very well, realised that Willie was already plotting, planning and scheming.

"Yes," continued Willie, "we'll need Jamie. See if they've a room at the Gamekeeper's Arms. We'll pay for everything and give him a few quid besides. And you and I must have a session on the practice ground. I've an idea that might help you a lot." He had the vacant look again and Sean slipped quietly out. At times like this Willie was best left alone.

Sean went home far happier. He knew what his friend was like. He knew how clever he was. He knew Julian would get his come-uppance. Sean chuckled. He wondered what scheme Willie would dream up. It was sure to be something good! Poor Julian! He almost felt sorry for him but he was so unkind he deserved all he got. Yet if Sean had known what would happen to Julian he would have been very sorry for him. Anybody would! But Sean never dreamt of the ruthlessness of the plot which was, at that moment, being hatched, or imagined the humiliation which Julian would suffer in front of those whose opinions he valued most. It was cruel, yes, but in Willie's view necessary. Julian should have known better than to cross swords with the old guard. When the chips are down they fight as dirty as the next man, perhaps even dirtier!

When Julian Prince walked into the bar lounge a few days later he saw the Three Wise Men sitting at their usual table in the window. Ever since he'd been so outspoken a few days earlier he'd regretted it for he knew that these worthy gentlemen still had a great deal of influence at the club, particularly when it came to picking future captains and presidents. Julian dearly wanted to be captain of the club. He yearned for the authority, the power, the social prestige that this office would bring. And it would be so good for business. He could entertain customers at the club and invite a favoured few to play golf with him. He was sure he'd make many valuable contacts. Julian ran a small engineering workshop and, although outwardly successful, it had in fact been badly hit by the recession. The future was very uncertain indeed. But if he were captain that would make all the difference. He was sure of it.

At the Black Hills Golf Club the vice-captain and vice-president for the coming year are chosen in great secrecy by the appropriate committee of past captains or past presidents. All three Wise Men had been both captains and presidents and so sat on both committees. Their opinions carried a great deal of weight. It was also known that, although most captains and presidents had been members for many years, very occasionally newish members were invited to take office as vice-captain if, for some reason, they were particularly popular. It was on this that Julian was banking. At the next committee meeting he intended to offer the club a footbridge to span the ravine at the 18th hole. For years tired golfers had struggled down the ravine in front of the 18th tee, then had to climb up the other side. A footbridge would do away with all that. It would certainly be popular – and so would he! He'd thought about it and reckoned he could get it constructed fairly cheaply through his contacts. He'd have to borrow some money but it would be an investment which would, he was confident, bring many future dividends. First, however, he had to make his peace with the Three Wise Men. He walked over to their table.

"Would you gentlemen care for a drink?" he offered.

Horace looked up balefully and nodded almost imperceptibly to the barman. Then he turned away to wave to Sean and Willie who were passing the window on their way to the first tee. They were dressed as usual, Willie with a collar and tie, Sean wearing an old waterproof jacket beneath which braces could be seen holding up baggy tweed trousers. Julian couldn't resist a dig at them.

"Getting past it aren't they?" he commented. "Looks as if they buy their clothes at Oxfam! They remind me of those old photographs you see of golfers like Harry Vardon. Pity they can't play like him." He guffawed unkindly.

"They still play pretty well," said Wilfred. "They've got to the semi-final of the Four Ball you know and I for one won't be surprised if they win it."

"Mitchell Binns and I play them in the next round," said Julian. "We're not expecting any problems," he added dismissively. "Should all be over pretty quickly. Don't know how they've got this far."

"Willie's got a bad back, you should win," muttered Horace sadly.

"I'd put money on Willie and Sean even if Willie has got a bad back," added Wilfred stoutly. "Those two can still play pretty good golf when they want to."

"Sean's got a bad shoulder," stated Horace gloomily. "Had three cortisone injections already but they haven't done a scrap of good. I believe he's been told to rest it but he won't stop playing golf. Feels he might never start again." He sipped his gin and tonic thoughtfully, reflecting sadly on the problems of growing old.

"Well I think we should be able to beat those two cripples," said Julian unfeelingly. He was getting very bored with Sean's and Willie's ailments.

"Bet you can't!" piped up the second oldest of the Three Wise Men who rarely spoke unless it was to order something from the barman or the stewardess.

"Pardon!" exclaimed Julian.

"Bet you can't!" repeated Herbert. "You think you're so bloody good don't you. Well put your money where your mouth is. I think they'll beat you easily!"

"They bloody well won't!" replied Julian, now exceedingly irritated. "They haven't got a hope."

"What odds'll you give me then?" enquired Herbert to the apparent astonishment of the other two veterans who gazed at him in disbelief.

"I'll give you a hundred to one," replied Julian stoutly, stung by the persistence of the elderly one.

"Done!" said Herbert quickly. "Geoff!" And he motioned the barman over. "Geoff, will you hold the stakes? Mr Prince and I are having a little bet."

"Certainly sir," agreed the barman. "And how much are you wanting to bet?"

"Oh I don't know," replied Herbert. "I'll just see what's in my jacket pocket". He began to fish out a collection of small coins and fluff from his pocket.

Now, just for a moment Julian experienced a chill of fear. It was as if a cold finger fleetingly touched his spine. He shivered. There was, after all, a remote chance that he might lose his bet. But when he looked at Herbert in

his shabby clothes and saw him assembling a variety of 1p and 2p pieces on the table, his confidence returned.

"Tell you what," he said, "if you bet all the money you've got in your jacket pocket I'll give you a hundred to one that Mitch and I'll beat Sean and Willie in the semi-final."

"How much have you got Herbert?" enquired Horace, suddenly interested in this offer.

"I don't know yet," replied the second Wise Man. "Just give me a minute."

He removed a button from his pocket which he stared at for several moments before examining his jacket to see whether one was missing. Then, feeling deep down into the furthest recesses of his pocket he brought out a tightly-folded note which he dropped casually on the table before continuing the search for more coins.

Julian looked at this. The cold finger had become an icy hand that held his heart in a vice-like grip. He found it difficult to breathe. Who'd have expected the old fool to have a bank-note in his jacket pocket!

"What's that note Herbert?" enquired Horace with interest, leaning forward to inspect it more closely.

"I'll tell you in a minute, just be patient can't you," replied Herbert rather irritably, attempting to unfold the note with arthritic fingers that wouldn't grasp the paper.

"Allow me sir," said Geoff, leaning over and nimbly unfolding the note.

"Good God Herbert, it's fifty quid!" exclaimed Horace.

"Fifty quid!" repeated Julian weakly.

"Fifty quid," stated Geoff firmly, whistling through his teeth.

There was a pregnant silence as the implication dawned on those present.

"That means, doesn't it, that if Sean and Willie win you'll owe Herbert £5,000?" enquired Horace speaking slowly but very distinctly.

"No! No! No!" replied Herbert, "that's not right at all."

"I quite agree with Herbert," said Julian, hurriedly grasping his opportunity like a drowning man a straw. "Not fifty quid! We ought to say fifty pen ..." But before he could finish Horace interrupted him again,

"Sorry!" he said. "Silly me! Of course it's not fifty quid. It's 50 quid and 27 pence. So if Sean and Willie win you'll owe Herbert £5027. That's the correct amount isn't it Geoff?"

"Yes sir," agreed the barman. "Quite correct sir." And he quickly swept all the coins and the note into his left hand and returned to the bar.

"Well Julian, this is exciting isn't it," said Wilfred gleefully. "It's lucky Sean and Willie haven't got a chance! I must say it's jolly sporting of you to offer odds like that. Adds a spot of interest to the proceedings it does by Jove. Jolly good show! Good luck to both teams I say."

There was a murmur of approval from the little group which had, by now, gathered round the table. And the Three Wise Men raised their glasses and drank to Julian's health with great gusto.

After that it was quite impossible for Julian to back out and he had to derive what comfort he could from the thought that there was really no possibility of him losing the match. If he'd seen what went on in the bar lounge after he'd left he might have felt less happy. The Three Wise Men were rocking with glee and shaking hands with each other, and Herbert wrote a note and left it behind the bar to be handed to Willie immediately he got in. It said very simply, 'FISH HOOKED'.

But fortunately Julian did not know all this. He did not realise that he was no longer master of his own destiny and was now simply a puppet on a string, dancing to someone else's tune, powerless to resist the events devised with such cunning by Willie Bradley.

Even so, Julian drove home in a state of shock. He couldn't believe what had happened. Two hours previously he'd kissed his wife goodbye and told her he was off to the club for a quiet drink. Then he hadn't a care in the world and now he was returning home and somehow – somehow – so quickly, so easily, he might lose £5,000. And he didn't have £5,000 to lose! His cash flow situation was very bad at the moment and there was no way the bank manager would allow him to increase his overdraft. How had it happened? Why on earth had he made that stupid bet? Why couldn't he have kept quiet! And whoever had £50 notes, forgotten, in their jacket pocket? That was unbelievable! Well he must be sensible. He must tell those old buggers that he didn't want to bet so much. It was silly! It was only a game after all. They'd understand. He might lose a bit of face but it would be worth it and very few people would know what had happened. Yes, that's what he'd do. He wouldn't go back now; there'd be too many people around. He'd go back at lunchtime tomorrow. The three of them'd be there then. They always were. He felt much happier now that he'd made the decision. There was no point in saying anything to his wife; she was always saying he talked too much. She need never know anything about it. When he got home he was his old cheerful self and he almost managed to forget what had happened. But he spent a restless night, sleeping little, tossing and turning, and wishing he'd returned to the club and sorted it all out.

It was coffee time at work the next morning when the call came through from the president.

"Julian old chap," he boomed, for he always shouted down the telephone, " I've just had a chat with the captain and he's told me about the little bet you've got with Herbert Hartley. Splendid! Apparently Herbert's said that if he wins he'll give the money to the club. He doesn't want it you know, he's very wealthy. I wondered if you'd care to do the same if you win? We could put your £50 into the centenary fund if you're agreeable. What d'ye say? It'd be a nice gesture old chap!"

But Julian was speechless and could only splutter incoherently. The president took this as agreement and pressed on happily.

" Well done old chap," he shouted, "knew you'd agree! Said to old Horace you were the right sort of chap for the club. Be captain one day shouldn't wonder! Have to go now, another of those blasted committee meetings."

He rang off and grinned at Willie who was sitting next to him in the secretary's office.

"You're a devious old bugger," he said," involving me in your wicked schemes. But there aren't many people I don't like and he's one of them. He's so arrogant. Thinks he owns the club! Needs taking down a peg or two! But he's a good golfer you know; you and Sean'll have a real battle on your hands. D'ye think ye can win?"

"There is a chance," replied Willie quietly, with a little smile. And there was a cold calculating look in his eyes that made the president decide that, whatever else came up, there was no way he was going to miss this match. He didn't know what Willie had up his sleeve but there was something – as sure as God made little green apples there was something. Well, he'd done his bit; he'd been asked to ring Julian and he'd done it. He wouldn't ask about anything else. He didn't want to know.

That same afternoon Willie met Sean on the practice ground. They had waited until no one else was around, and even then had walked to the far end where they were hidden by large rhododendron bushes. Sean had his clubs but Willie carried only a hold-all. They looked round carefully to see that the coast was clear before Willie removed an orange life-jacket from the bag. He helped Sean put it on. It took a little while to push Sean's arms through the inflatable sleeves and fasten the straps around his waist. Willie then took out a foot pump and carefully pumped up the life-jacket. The air filled the sleeves and Sean's arms rose gradually, further and further. He looked like a Michelin man.

"Try swinging!" ordered Willie, giving Sean his driver. Sean grasped the club tightly and tried a practice swing. The jacket slowed his movements down considerably. He could not get his hands above waist height on the backswing.

"Too much air!" decided Willie, letting some out.

"Better," said Sean, swinging back smoothly and almost reaching the top of his normal backswing. "It needs more air out yet, though." Sean could now almost take a full swing, a swing that was much slower and smoother than normal.

"This is no good," he said in disgust, "Oi'm swingin' far too slowly, the club's hardly moving!"

"Your backswing's still fast," replied Willie firmly. "I'm putting a bit more air in." And so saying he inflated the life-jacket a little further. "Now," he said, "we'll try hitting a ball."

Sean still had grave misgivings. When Willie had pointed out that he always played his best on cold wet winter days when he had all his waterproofs on, he had been forced to agree. And when Willie had reasoned that this was because the clothes slowed down his naturally fast swing, he hadn't argued. But this was ridiculous! The life-jacket slowed his swing down to such an extent that he felt the ball would go no distance! He waited impatiently whilst Willie teed up a ball. He couldn't bend down himself with this silly jacket on. He felt such a fool!

"Now, just keep your eye on the ball and swing normally," ordered Willie sternly.

Sean shook his head, had a practice swing and addressed the ball. The club moved smoothly back until the shaft was nearly horizontal. After a slight pause the downswing began and the club head accelerated, travelling faster and faster as it approached the ball. There was a sharp satisfying crack as impact was made. The ball shot away as if jet-propelled, climbing higher and higher as it flew over a distant copse of trees.

"Wow!" said Sean.

"Bloody Hell!" exclaimed Willie. "What a shot!"

"Oi didn't feel that Oi'd hit the ball at all," muttered Sean. "The club seemed to be moving so slowly Oi didn't think the ball would go anywhere."

They spent the next hour experimenting with different clubs. The improvement in Sean's shotmaking was dramatic. His iron shots flew straight and true; no longer did he have the duck hook that usually characterised his game. He had never hit his woods so far. After an hour he was exhausted and very, very hot.

"Oi'll have to take this jacket off Willie," he gasped, perspiration streaming down his face, "Oi'm completely knackered!"
Willie let the air out and undid the straps around Sean's waist. His shirt was wet through. Willie was concerned.

"I hope it's not as warm as this on the day of the match," he said, "because you'll have to wear a thick pullover on top of this jacket to hide it. I shouldn't think it's legal. It probably counts as 'unusual equipment' because it assists you in making a stroke."

"Well," said Sean happily, " if it's necessary to wear it in order to beat Julian Oi'll put up with it. Oi haven't hit shots like those for years. It's one way of losing weight anyway!"
The two returned to the clubhouse well satisfied with their morning's work.

Julian, however, spent an uncomfortable ten days before the match. Of course the news had quickly got round the club. His partner had rung up the next day to tell him what a fool he was. Mitchell had been a member much longer than Julian. He knew what went on at the club and how much influence certain senior members still had. And, as he pointed out to Julian, Sean and Willie had reached the semi-final and beaten some strong partnerships so they must be pretty good! Over the years he'd been a member Mitch had heard some very strange stories about Willie Bradley. He'd won some matches when nobody had given him a chance. No, Mitch would do his very best, and get in as much practice as he could before the match, but he was glad it wasn't his five grand at stake!

These were not the sort of remarks to generate confidence and Julian was rather rattled. There were, on the other hand, the phone calls from the Friday leaguers, the elite band of serious golfers who, each week, took part in silent intense matches against similar players from other clubs. They were superior beings, much admired by Julian and they had, almost to a man, been fulsome in their praise for his brave and spirited wager. He felt better when he thought of them. One had even suggested there might be a place for him on the team.

So, as the day of the match approached, his mood changed frequently. One minute he felt a hero – a man's man, a chap who walked tall, unafraid of a challenge. The next, he knew he was an idiot, a fool who'd gambled an incredible amount of money on a game of golf. Usually it was worst about 2.30 in the mornings when, bathed in perspiration, he was having yet another sleepless night endlessly going over it all.

He did what he could. He practised hard. He often visited the local driving range. Undoubtedly he was hitting the ball better. He was sure they'd win.

It was a relief when the day of the contest dawned. He decided to dress flamboyantly. Whatever happened he would be remembered for his dignity, his smartness, his presence. He'd show them all. He would win – no question about it! He was touched when his wife suggested he wore the birthday present she'd given him a few days earlier. Women were funny! Debbie had been so unreasonable about the match until now, but now she clearly wanted him to win.

The match was scheduled to begin at two o'clock. At 1.30 the car park was full. At 1.45 over a hundred members surrounded the first tee. Others stood around the putting green. At 1.50 Julian and Mitchell arrived.

There was applause and many comments such as, "Ooo doesn't he look lovely!" And "Who's your friend Mitch?" For Julian was dressed all in yellow, pale yellow slacks and a greeny-yellow tee-shirt. Even his shoes – top-of-the-range Footjoys – were yellow and black. Julian had chosen the ensemble with care. He knew there would be a large gallery for the match. He knew that many of the young bloods at the club greatly admired him for his bet and he was determined to create a memorable impression. He was smiling. There was no way he could lose! Mitchell wore the blue trousers, blue tee-shirt and blue pullover that he always wore.

At five minutes to two a strange trio approached the first tee. Sean and Willie walked together, slightly in front of the third man who limped respectfully two paces behind, carrying a golf-bag on each shoulder. Willie was dressed in his usual clothes although his tie was perhaps a shade brighter than usual. Sean was wearing an old baseball cap and his favourite trousers. It was a warm day but he also had on several bulky pullovers and looked very round and plump.

"Sean's put on a lot of weight," commented the secretary to the president.

The applause which greeted the elderly pair gave way to gasps of amazement as their caddie came into view. He was a small man but immensely broad. He wore a tweed jacket over a string vest and silver grey trousers which tapered sharply and were fastened with bicycle clips above hobnailed boots. But it was his face, his battered squashed face that caused some to whistle in amazement and others to turn away in embarrassment. He followed Sean and Willie onto the tee and stood waiting silently for the action to begin. A powerful smell of alcohol wafted around the spectators.

From the outset it was Sean who dominated the game. Never had he played so well; never had he hit the ball so far. He was swinging slowly and smoothly although not without effort. Indeed from his red face and the perspiration that dripped from him it was obvious that he was putting a great deal of effort into his shots, yet his swing was amazingly slow and his timing superb. He reached the first green, a short par five, in two shots, and two putts gave him a gross birdie and his side an easy win.

The second hole is considered by many to be the most difficult par four on the course, requiring as it does a long carry to the green, with the second shot over a ravine filled with rough grass, bushes, trees and heather, picturesque but frightening, and the reason why many medal cards are torn up early on in a round. Julian, Mitchell and Willie played conservatively left, relying on a pitch and one putt for their pars. Sean went straight for the green and his five wood shot flew straight and true, high above all the trouble, finishing on the green.
"Wonderful shot Sean!" called out the president.
"Thank you Norman," replied Sean politely, mopping his brow.
"Why don't you take a sweater off?" enquired the president. "You look very warm."
"Oi'm all right. Oi'm fine," gasped Sean. "There's a sneaky wind you know. Oi don't want to catch a chill."
"Well you're the doctor, you should know best," muttered the president, "but I can't feel any wind at all!"

After three holes Sean and Willie were two in front. At the fourth, a par five, Mitch holed a long putt for a birdie to halve the hole. Sean already had a five nett four. At the fifth Julian got a birdie but it was no use for Sean hit two magnificent shots nearly onto the green and chipped close enough to

get his own gross birdie, nett eagle. The standard of golf was exceptional and the gallery applauded vigorously as each good shot was played. The sixth is a tricky par four, a dog-leg with out-of-bounds on the left. Sean rifled a long tee shot around the corner, then played a four iron to the heart of the green and holed the putt for yet another birdie. Four up!

Mitch walked with Julian towards the seventh tee. "This is extraordinary," he said. "Unbelievable! Nicklaus himself couldn't play as well as Sean. I've never seen anything like it. If they carry on like this we're sunk. It'll all be over by the 12th!"

Julian was very pale. He said nothing. What was there to say? Or do? He and Mitch were playing well, as well as they could, yet they were four down already and there were no signs of weakness in the opposition. Disaster stared him in the face. Ruin. He groaned. What could he do?

The seventh is a short hole down a hillside from an elevated tee to a green around which the beck flows swiftly, waiting to capture the bold shot or one which is off-line. Sean always had a pee at the seventh. The brambles and gorse bushes alongside the tee provided ideal cover. Today of all days he felt a pressing need to go.

"Excuse me a moment," he said.

Gingerly he began to climb down the slippery slope at the side of the tee, looking at the ground intently, carefully choosing the next place to put his foot. Julian stood at the side of the tee watching him and, all of a sudden, a most unsportsmanlike thought came into his mind. If only the old fool would slip and break his arm, or his wrist, or even a finger, that would be enough! Sean was playing so well they were almost certain to lose and then he'd be finished. He hadn't got £5,000; he hadn't even got £500! What a mess!

At that moment a large heron flew across the fairway, languidly winging its way to the beck behind the green. With all eyes on the bird Julian saw his chance. He pushed his heavy golf-bag sideways. It hit Sean who lost his balance and fell headlong into the middle of the gorse bushes.

"My goodness! Are you all right?" enquired Julian rushing to help him up. "I do hope you haven't broken anything. I'm very sorry about my clubs. I just let go of them for a second whilst I was watching that damn bird and they fell on you. It was awfully bad luck. I'm so sorry!"

Sean staggered to his feet. He was white. He looked thinner – much thinner – almost deflated. Willie walked quickly over and, as he got near, heard a faint hissing sound. He took Sean by the arm and quickly led him to the back of the tee.

"Are you all right?" he asked anxiously.

"Oi'm all right," muttered Sean. "But that was no accident! That bugger threw his golf-bag at me! It was quite deliberate. Oi saw him out of the corner of my eye. He was trying to nobble me and Oi think he bloody well has, the bloody jacket's punctured!"

"Right!" said Willie. "Don't worry." And there was a cold steeliness in his voice that boded ill for the opposition. "If that's how he wants to play it – OK! I didn't want to, but we may have to use Jamie." He moved away to speak to the caddie, who listened intently, nodding several times.

Willie suggested they should have a short break and a cup of coffee at that point. He'd brought a flask. It would help Sean get over his fall. Julian and Mitchell readily agreed. Julian was pleased to be offered a cup and thanked Willie profusely. He was very relieved to have got away with his ploy. Obviously they didn't suspect a thing and there was no doubt Sean looked very shaken even though he hadn't broken anything. Funny how he'd fallen so softly on that bush; it was so gentle it had been almost like falling on a cushion! Julian chatted away cheerfully. He felt sure Sean would be put off his game by that fall. It didn't need much to put you off at golf! He had a feeling that things would go his way now. Yes, he felt sure of it!

Jamie refused a coffee. Instead he produced a hip flask from an inside pocket and had a long drink with great enjoyment. And then another! As they left the tee he started humming to himself, making a curious wailing sound that Julian found disturbing. He was never sure when it would get louder and sometimes it was at its loudest when he was playing his shots.

Sean's game deteriorated after his accident. Without doubt it had upset him. He seemed ill at ease, and those watching commented that he was swinging much faster and his rhythm wasn't nearly so good. They put it down to the fall. Willie managed a three at the seventh but they both made a complete mess of the eighth and ninth so their lead was down to two.

Jamie had taken to having a drink from his flask on each tee and, on the tenth, drank long and deeply, finishing the contents of the flask. He had become much noisier now, singing to himself in a throaty gargle and often coughing with a horrid phlegmy sound. On this tee he had difficulty removing the head cover from Sean's driver. When he finally got it off he handed Sean the club and then bent down, ferreting around inside Sean's golf-bag. After a while he found a new bottle of whisky, unscrewed the cap and again drank deeply. Then he belched loudly.

"Your bloody caddie's drunk!" exclaimed Julian in disgust. "You shouldn't have allowed it."

"Not Jamie," replied Sean. "Jamie never gets drunk, do you Jamie?" His caddie swayed alarmingly and put a huge hand on Sean's shoulder to steady himself.

"Derrrunk?" he spluttered. "Och, no! Ah'mm nivver derrrunk!" And so saying he overbalanced and a large boot landed heavily on Julian's foot, crushing his beautiful shoe and causing him excruciating pain.

"You bloody fool!" he shouted, hopping about in agony. "You've ruined these shoes. A hundred quid they were! You'll have to pay for another pair. I think you've broken several toes you bloody moron!"

"Calm down Julian," said Sean. "It was an accident and accidents can happen as you very well know. Sit down on this seat and let me have a look at your foot. Oi'll buy you another pair of shoes."

Julian limped over to the seat and sat down, moaning occasionally as Sean removed the damaged shoe and examined his foot carefully, getting him to wiggle each toe in turn.

"Ye're all right," he announced. "Nothing's broken. Bit of bruising though, ye'll find it's black and blue tomorrow Julian, and Oi expect it'll swell up a bit, but nothing to worry about, nothing's broken. Ye'll be right as rain in a week or so."

He then turned to his caddie, "Jamie," he said sternly, "be much more careful in future and, if ye're going to fall over, try to avoid hitting anybody, ye might hurt them. Now come and apologise to Mr Prince."

The caddie, looking very crestfallen, lurched over to Julian and offered him a drink from the bottle of whisky.

"Ye'll tak' a dram wi' mi?" he asked, "shoo' the's nay hard feelin'." He undid the bottle cap and wiped the top on his dirty sleeve before thrusting it into Julian's face.

Julian glanced up at Jamie glowering over him and decided it was wisest not to refuse even though he didn't fancy drinking from the same bottle as

Jamie. But Jamie looked so threatening, leering down at him, that he took the bottle and drank a small amount before giving it back to the caddie, who grabbed it quickly.

"Ye'll fee' better noo," stated that gentleman indistinctly. "Ah'll mebbe tak' a wee dram wi' ye. A man shouldna' derrink on his ain."

Once more he drank deeply from the bottle, the whisky level dropping alarmingly.

Sean had been examining Julian's shoe carefully and had managed to push out the leather at the toe so that it was wearable – damaged irreparably but wearable. When he looked up and saw Jamie standing by Julian, drinking from the bottle, he hurried over.

"Whatever ye do," he whispered to Julian, "whatever ye do, don't drink from Jamie's whisky bottle. It wouldn't be wise at all."

"You're too late, I just have," replied Julian. "Why not anyway? I don't suppose it'll do me any harm, not as much as having that bloody gorilla jumping on my foot anyway!"

"Ah!' said Sean. "Oh dear! Oh dear! Oh dear! What a shame! A dreadful shame! Oi wasn't in time to warn ye. Oi should've … But never mind. It'll probably be all right. It's not very catching. Nothing we can do now anyway." He walked away shaking his head and Julian saw him speaking sternly to the caddie.

Julian replaced the wreck of his shoe and limped slowly and painfully over to Sean.

"Why shouldn't I have drunk from that bottle of Jamie's?" he asked. "What's the matter with him?"

"Nothing to worry about at all," said Sean. He went on quickly and Julian got the distinct impression he was trying to convince himself. "Much better not to know about these things anyway, it'd only worry you – quite unnecessarily of course," he added hastily. "You might not catch anything, probably won't, almost certainly not in fact, and even if you do it will be a long time before ..."

He stopped abruptly and patted Julian's arm comfortingly, putting on the brave smile he'd used in the past when he wanted to strike terror into the heart of one of his patients. Julian was disturbed. He felt very uneasy. What on earth was wrong with that bloody caddie. It couldn't be anything really serious could it? Surely not. This was England after all, not Bangkok. He took his handkerchief out of his pocket and rubbed his lips hard. His foot ached abominably. He began to feel very hot.

It was fortunate for Julian that his partner, who had been playing steadily if unspectacularly during the first nine holes, should suddenly have a purple patch. Mitch could do nothing wrong; perfect shot followed perfect shot. A par at the 10th was followed by a two at the short 11th. Another birdie at the 12th was followed by a par at the 13th. On the 14th tee the match was all square and, whilst Mitch was making these Herculean efforts, Julian was listless, uninterested even, a shadow of his former self. The worry he had felt about losing his money had been replaced now by thoughts of perhaps losing his life. He was convinced that Jamie had passed on some unspeakable illness, some disease so dreadful that he would soon die and all his hopes and plans for the future would come to naught. He got the feeling that both Sean and Willie were treating him with much more kindness than they had hitherto, with sympathy even, as if they knew what lay in store. He kept well away from Jamie who was becoming noisier by the minute and brought out the whisky bottle several times on each hole.

On the 14th tee Julian suddenly decided that whatever was in store for him he might as well enjoy what little time he had left. He thumped his drive hard and it shot away down the middle of the fairway, well in front of anybody else's. As they walked down the slope from the tee Jamie stumbled and nearly fell. Willie caught him and helped him down the fairway. He mumbled something to Willie who talked to him in a low voice for several minutes as they walked to the drives. Willie was obviously concerned about Jamie. He had a long discussion with Sean and then asked Julian and Mitch if they'd mind having a short break on the next tee as he had another flask of coffee in his golf-bag and thought a cup would do Jamie good as the caddie wasn't feeling so well.

"No problem," agreed Mitch, smiling.

"He's just drunk!" muttered Julian. "It's disgusting!" But he hadn't the heart to argue.

Sean made a complete mess of the 14th and, in the end, Willie had to hole a tricky five-footer downhill, left to right borrow, in order to halve the hole. Both Sean and Willie looked grey and drawn as they walked slowly to the 15th tee.

"Getting very tired aren't they," the little secretary whispered to the president. "It looks as if the centenary committee'll have to whistle for the five grand after all."

"Don't be too sure," replied the president. "My money's still on Sean and Willie. You never know what'll happen with that pair."

Little did the president know how prophetic were his words. On the 15th tee Willie took a large flask from his golf-bag, unscrewed the top and gave it to Jamie to hold. Jamie was very unsteady now, swaying backwards and forwards in an alarming manner. Willie put a hand on his arm to steady him and filled a cup with steaming black coffee.

"Drink that Jamie," he ordered, "it'll make you feel better. But be careful it's very hot."

He let go of Jamie's arm and turned away to pour a cup for Sean. In that instant Jamie lost his balance completely and fell forwards, throwing boiling coffee down the front of Julian's trousers. Julian danced away, shouting with shock and pain as the hot liquid soaked through the lightweight trousers and reached delicate parts of a personal and sensitive nature.

"You bloody idiot!" he screamed. "You stupid bloody fool! Look what you've done! You've ruined these trousers and ..." He stopped and cried out in agony as the hot coffee penetrated even further.

"Julian!" said Sean very firmly, "Take your trousers off immediately before any damage is done. We must pour something cold over your old man. Oi've got a bottle of cold water in my golf bag. That'll do! Come on now. Hurry up and get those trousers off. We don't want you injured."

"I bloody well am injured!" yelled Julian. "Your caddie, your bloody drunken caddie half crippled me and now he's thrown boiling coffee at me. He's not safe to have around. He ought to be locked up," he moaned as the steaming coffee dripped down his legs.

"Take your trousers off now!" ordered Sean in his best GP manner. "Now! Hurry up man. No time to be shy!"

He was starting to get a little worried, Julian was making such a noise, but maybe it was just shock. They had checked the temperature of the coffee carefully in the clubhouse before the match and it must have cooled down a bit whilst they were playing. Yes, it would just be shock. Julian seemed very reluctant to take his trousers off though and he didn't know why.

Julian knew. He had a problem! A week ago it had been his birthday and his wife, trying to cheer him up, had bought him a pair of particularly striking boxer shorts as a present. They were pink and covered in red hearts, with little Cupids firing arrows. And the awful thing was that in big bold letters across the front it said 'WHO'S A BIG BOY THEN'. His wife had laughed. Julian had laughed – at the time! But he'd not worn them – not till today! Today of all days his wife had suggested he put them on to bring him luck, make him feel good. Today of all days. Of all the bloody, bloody, bad luck!

Slowly Julian undid his belt. Slowly he took off the stained, dripping trousers. There was some clapping and then laughter as the shorts were revealed and those nearby read the message.

"Get those shorts off as well Julian," ordered Sean, trying to keep a straight face. Really, he reflected, things had turned out remarkably well. "Come on now, hurry up, we'll stand in front of you."

Julian slowly removed his shorts. He felt totally humiliated. A laughing stock. This would never be forgotten; he knew it! He stood mutely, his spirit crushed, as Sean poured cold water over him. He looked up and saw the president trying hard not to laugh. He heard someone say that it wasn't true what was written on the shorts and he heard shouts of laughter. Mitch, even Mitch, was smiling broadly. Julian stood quite still and the cold water dripped down everywhere. Sean straightened up.

"That should do the trick," he said. "You'll be all right now." And then he went on very quietly so that only Julian could hear. "This is even worse than changing shoes in the car park don't you think – taking your trousers off on the course. We'll have to ask the committee if it's against the rules."

Julian's mouth fell open. He gazed wide-eyed at Sean. Then he looked at Willie talking to the caddie who didn't seem to be swaying at all now. And he knew. They'd arranged it all. They'd planned everything – the crafty old buggers! But he'd never be able to prove it. No way. Everybody'd just think he was a bad sport. The buggers, the devious, scheming, conniving old buggers. But what could he do? He hadn't even any trousers to wear. No-one would ever take him seriously again.

At that moment Willie ambled up with an old pair of waterproof trousers.

"These any good?" he enquired. "Borrow them if you like." And he handed them to Julian. Julian put them on. They were very short and did not reach his ankles. They were also far too large. The only way he could keep them up was to hold the waistband with his left hand. He felt like a tramp with his battered shoe and the dirty trousers.

"Thank you," he said politely, "most kind." He looked round once again and saw all the smiling faces. They were really enjoying this he could tell. Even Mitch. They were pleased at what'd happened. He hated them all! He wanted to get away from everybody – far, far away – and never come back! "You can have the match," he told Sean. In complete silence he picked up his bag and shuffled back to the clubhouse. Alone.

"Didn't even shake hands!" muttered old Horace as the rest of them walked slowly back.

At lunchtime next day the president parked his car in his special parking space and slowly made his way through the clubhouse to the bar lounge. He was thinking deeply, planning what to say. As he'd expected, the Three Wise Men were sitting at their usual table and Sean and Willie were there too, deep in conversation. They all looked up as he approached – rather guiltily he thought.

"Afternoon Mr President, nice to see you," said Sean. "Ye'll have your usual?" he enquired.

"Yes thank you," replied the president. He pulled up another chair and sat down. For a few moments there was silence. Then he spoke, "Had a phone call late last night," he said, "from Julian. Told me he'd decided to resign from the club. Doesn't feel he fits in somehow. Going to sell his business to pay the bet. Has to do it. Says there's no other way. Point of honour to pay of course. Did my best to persuade him not to resign. Told him what a lot of good work he'd done for the club on the committee. But it was no use, he'd quite made up his mind."

The president stopped and sipped his gin and tonic thoughtfully. No-one spoke. After a little while the president continued, "Well," he said, "I don't know what you think but I think Julian's had a pretty rough ride. I know he can be a bit objectionable at times and isn't very popular amongst certain older members, but I reckon he's been nobbled! I don't know how – and I don't want to know – but thinking it over I feel he got more than he deserved. Anyway I told Julian that if he wanted to leave the club I'd quite understand but I also said that in view of the circumstances – in view of the very strange circumstances – I would suggest – strongly suggest to you Herbert, that the bet should be cancelled. What d'ye say?" The second oldest of the Three Wise Men slowly took out of his pocket a piece of paper. It had several names written on it. He drew a line through the one at the top of the list.

"Yes Mr President," he said. "I quite agree."

HOT BALLS

In which technology triumphs but sportsmanship prevails.

W illie Bradley sat quite still in his favourite armchair, his brow furrowed, his demeanour grave. He felt despondent, dejected. Life was no longer the happy, carefree existence that a man with his income and good health had every right to expect. Outside it was warm and sunny. One or two birds were singing. His wife Sue, of whom he was very fond, was doing a spot of heavy digging in the vegetable patch. In short God was in his Heaven and all seemed right with the world. But not so! A large black cloud hung over Willie, a cloud with a name – Sydney Sunter, or Hissin' Syd as he was known at the golf club on account of his teeth. Willie was very cross with Syd and the frustrating thing was that he couldn't think what to do about it. His one-time friend Syd had touched a raw nerve and Willie felt humiliated.

It had all started the day before. He had been playing a friendly golf match against Syd. Willie was playing very well and, with three holes to go, was two up. "Ahaaa!" I hear you say knowingly, "two up and three to play never wins. It's a well known fact." But when you are in that position you always feel you will win, and most people do. However Syd won the 16th by holing a monstrously long putt and then, at the short 17th, had a tremendous stroke of luck because his tee shot dropped in a bunker, then bounced out onto the green – something that never happens except to the other person when he's playing you in a match. And of course Syd holed that putt also, for a birdie two.

So the match was all square and the atmosphere tense, for senior golfers take these games pretty seriously. It was Syd to drive first at the 18th. He threw several bits of grass into the air to check for wind speed and direction. (There wasn't any wind at all; it was one of those breathless days. He was just delaying things as Willie well knew.) Then he gazed immobile down the fairway for several minutes like Jack Nicklaus does, to compose himself. (Why did he need to compose himself, Willie thought. He'd just won two holes he shouldn't have won and was now delaying things to make Willie even more irritated.) Then he hit a quite magnificent drive down the centre of the fairway. It was one of those drives that all golfers hit about once every two years when all their faults are somehow cancelled out and the result is a perfectly timed shot. Syd's ball went off like a rocket and came to rest within easy reach of the green, about 220 yards from the tee.

"Great shot Syd," said Willie with genuine admiration.

"I've been hitting a lot like that lately," said Syd untruthfully. "That wasn't one of my best; you'll easily get in front of it."

Now Willie had played golf for many years and immediately recognized the *getting the opponent to press* ploy – well known even to amateur students of gamesmanship. He knew what Syd was up to. He knew Syd hadn't hit one like that for years. And he also knew he couldn't possibly get as far. Of course he should just have played an ordinary shot, perhaps even with a three wood to make sure of getting on for two. Probably he would then have won the hole. But of course he didn't. He was niggled. He was cross. It wasn't fair! Syd had just had three colossal strokes of luck. It damned well wasn't fair! So, human nature being what it is, he did what any red-blooded golfer would do, gripped the club far too tightly, swung back far too quickly and hooked his drive far out-of-bounds over the lane alongside the 18th fairway.

"Damn and blast!" said Willie with great feeling, searching for another ball.

"Hard luck," said Syd with great satisfaction and then went on, quite unnecessarily, "You wouldn't have done that a few years ago. I expect it's your age. You older chaps have got to accept that you can't play like you used to do."

That did it of course. It was offensive. It was uncalled-for. It was true! Willie was extremely irritated. He was only a year older than Syd. He'd always had a lower handicap. He was a better golfer than Syd too! Inevitably he lost the last hole and the match, and could only just bring himself to be civil afterwards during toasted tea-cakes in the clubhouse. Syd was cock-a-hoop. He suggested they had another game in a couple of weeks and of course Willie had to agree. When Syd went on to suggest that it might be a good idea if Willie had a few lessons beforehand he even managed a smile though seething inwardly. Something would have to be done so that he could beat that arrogant so-and-so. He'd like to crush him by at least six and five; that would take the smile off his face! But how? After all he was nearly 75 and must expect to lose length at his age. Perhaps he should just accept the inevitable.

"I will not", he said out loud in the car as he was driving home. "I'll show that cocky little bugger!"

When he got home and Sue enquired whether he'd enjoyed his game he was still ill-humoured enough to inform her that golf was far too serious a game to be enjoyed, except by ladies. The real problem was that, lately, he knew that he hadn't been hitting the ball as far as he used to do. So Syd had found his sensitive spot and hurt his pride. He thought about Syd's suggestion; perhaps he should have a lesson after all. There may be some little thing that he wasn't doing right which might make all the difference. But Willie remembered the last time he'd nearly had a lesson. He had been to a well-known and highly respected local professional who had won many tournaments and once played for Great Britain and Northern Ireland against America in the Ryder Cup. The Eminent One was a taciturn man in his 70s whom Willie felt would appreciate the problems of the senior golfer. The Eminent One, together with his pipe and black retriever, accompanied Willie to the practice ground where he teed up a ball for Willie, grunting twice to indicate that Willie should hit it. He did – very well he thought. The Eminent One said nothing but continued to tee up balls one after another which Willie duly hit. Nothing was said. Willie felt that he was striking the balls as well as he possibly could do and attributed the silence to the fact that the Eminent One was unable to spot any fault in his swing. After the sixth ball had sped away the Eminent One removed his pipe and spoke,

"Yerr swing is terrrible," he said. "Ah canna' help ye. Tha' shud tak' up baw's!"

And with that he whistled for his dog, replaced his pipe and set off back to the clubhouse. Willie had avoided professional advice ever since and now, on reflection, felt that he could expect no help from that quarter. No, he would have to sort it out himself. But how? What could he do?

So Willie Bradley sat and thought, and thought and sat, and nothing came to mind. And then, as so often happens on such occasions, he fell asleep. When he awoke he felt much refreshed and much happier, for a plan of action was forming in his mind. It was always the same, he reflected happily, you chew over a problem for ages without getting anywhere and then, if you just give them a chance, all of a sudden – zap! – the old grey cells come up with a winner. It was really very simple. If he couldn't improve his swing he'd have to improve his equipment, and there were only two possibilities, he'd either have to make the golf-balls fly further or he'd have to do something to his driver so that it would swing faster. He would start with the balls, that would be easier, and if that were not successful he would see what could be done to the clubs.

Quite unaware of what he was doing Willie got up and poured himself three fingers of Talisker. Totally relaxed now, sitting in his favourite armchair, he sipped the great malt and gave all his attention to the task in hand. How could he make a golf-ball go further without hitting it any harder; that was the problem!

One possibility was the cover. Perhaps if the dimples were deeper the ball would carry further in flight. But Willie soon rejected that. It would be too noticeable if he altered the cover; he'd never get away with it and, anyway, he felt sure it wouldn't have enough effect. No, the distance came from the core of the ball so it would be necessary to do something to make the core more elastic. But what? Well, what about temperature? The old pros always used to carry a spare ball in their trouser pocket, warming it up ready for the next hole. Did it really make much difference? And suppose a golf-ball was really hot; would it go much further then? Now was the time to find out.

Willie jumped up and shouted to Sue to come in from the garden. She arrived, breathless, a few minutes later.
"What on earth's the matter William?" she gasped.
"I need the egg pan dear," said Willie.
"It's where it always is," said Sue, exasperated, pointing to the article in question in its rack over the cooker. "Are you hungry William?"
"No, not at all," said Willie. "I just want to boil some golf-balls."
"Oh, that's all right then," said Sue, "because I would like to finish off the digging before lunch. It's too warm for digging in the afternoon."
"Don't let me stop you dear," said Willie, always a gentleman. "But before you go perhaps you'd be kind enough to fill the egg pan with water and put it on to boil."

He then went upstairs to the bedroom where he kept a collection of new golf-balls as well as several putters and a sawn-off snooker cue in case of burglars. He selected six Pinnacles, reasoning that the harder, solid balls

would be more susceptible to temperature changes. He went back to the kitchen and fastened a five foot tape-measure to the wall. He then fetched a roofing slate from the garage, placing it on the floor so that the bottom end of the tape-measure rested on the top surface of the slate. Then, very carefully, he dropped the six Pinnacles one after the other from the top of the tape-measure, watching to see how far up they bounced.

He was pleased to see that all six bounced up to about the same height – 48 inches on his tape-measure. Then he put the balls into the egg pan in boiling water and left them for 30 minutes, after which he thought they would have reached the temperature of the boiling water. Using a wooden spoon he removed each ball in turn and dropped them from the top of the tape measure. To his surprise the balls did not bounce as high as before and, when examined, he could see clearly the line where the two halves of the case had been joined together. It looked as if the case had expanded. Boiling water was, he decided, too hot.

Willie then found a thermometer in his workshop which would measure temperatures between 0°C and 100°C. By keeping the egg pan on a low light on the cooker, and carefully adding cold water to the pan which also had the golf-balls in it, Willie was able to test the rebound resilience of the balls at temperatures of 40°C, 60°C and 80°C. To his great satisfaction he found that 60°C was the best temperature, the balls then bouncing up to a height of more than 50 inches.

Willie left all the golf-balls in the refrigerator whilst he had a cup of coffee. It was important to check whether or not a temperature of 0°C would help. It didn't. The balls only bounced to 44 inches.

The message was clear – hot balls bounce best as long as they're not too hot. Now Willie was well aware that the situation would be different with a golf shot when the ball is hit hard and partially squashed by a club head travelling very quickly. Nonetheless he thought that hitting the ball hard, with a club, would enhance the temperature effect and make a hot ball travel much further than a cold one. He resolved to make a device which would warm up his golf-balls so that he always had a warm ball to drive with. This would be fairly simple. He could put two hand-warmers, together with several balls, inside an insulated box. If he replaced the ball he was playing with after every hole he would always have a warm ball for the next hole.

But Willie was disappointed. The improvement was not dramatic enough. He gained a few extra yards but not 50 or 100. That was what he really needed. He felt sure that if he could warm up the whole core of the ball rather than just the outside the effect would be far greater. Willie remembered an article in one of the golf magazines on the new Dunlop golf-ball. As far as he could remember this ball had a particularly thin dimpled cover of something called polyurethane and a larger than normal core of polybutadiene. The article said this was an advantage because the cores gave the distance and hence the larger the core the better. Clearly these were the balls to use. Now he thought some more about it he could see why the 100°C Pinnacles hadn't done so well. The covers had been very much hotter than the insides and would have expanded away from the cores, probably leaving a gap, which would be very undesirable as the energy from the club head would not be transferred efficiently to the core.

He had to find a way of heating up a ball from its centre, then the core would expand and press tightly against the case and all the energy from the club would be transmitted from cover to core. Willie went to the library to find the temperature at which the synthetic rubber cores bounced best. It was about 60°C just as his own tests had shown. Now all he had to do was find a way of heating up the cores from the inside. That would not be easy, very difficult in fact. He would have to consult George.

Willie Bradley and George Davidson had been friends for many years. Although now in his 70s George still loved to tinker with anything electrical and liked nothing better than a challenge. Willie drove over to see him and found him in his workshop. Willie explained his problem. George said nothing for a long time, quietly puffing on his pipe. Then he gave his opinion. It was going to be difficult, perhaps even impossible, to heat up the core of a golf-ball from the centre to 60°C in a short time. However Willie was not discouraged; he knew his friend too well. George told Willie to leave him six Dunlops and come back in a week on the off-chance that he had been able to think of something, but Willie should not raise his hopes too high, this was a tricky one!

During the following week Willie practised hard. Each day he visited the local driving range and concentrated on swinging slowly. Gradually his timing improved and, at the end of the week, he was far more consistent and his shots were going a good ten yards further. He could have practised at the club but did not wish to be seen practising. He had decided to give Syd a lesson he would never forget and it was vital that no-one suspected that he was taking the game seriously. No, he had to make them all believe that he hadn't been playing much, particularly Syd who played every day and never missed anything that was going on at the club. But it all depended on George. Could George come up trumps?

The following week Willie went to see George again. He arrived at George's house with many misgivings and a bottle of his friend's favourite whisky. He need not have worried. George opened the door and, without a word, beckoned him into his workshop. On the bench was a board containing three vertical spikes with rounded tips connected to a control box and a car battery. George showed Willie three balls, each of which had a fine hole drilled through the 'o' of Dunlop down to the centre of the core. Then, taking his pipe out of his mouth, George explained that the rounded tips were in fact small but extremely powerful heaters which, when inserted into a golf-ball, were quite capable of raising the temperature of the whole core to 60°C or above. The spikes also contained temperature sensors and the control box possessed two bulbs, one red, one green. After about half-an-hour, when the temperature had reached 60°C, the red light would go out and the green light would come on. However, and George emphasised how important this was, although the red light was no longer on, the heating would still continue for he had not had time to incorporate a heater cut-out. Therefore, unless the golf-ball was removed from the spike, its temperature would go on rising and high stresses would be produced in the core, which couldn't expand as much as it wanted to because of the case. The case would start to get pretty hot too. George didn't know what would happen if Willie hit a very hot ball except that he'd probably burn his fingers trying to tee it up.

Willie was delighted. He thanked his friend profusely, promising to return at a later date to report on the outcome of field trials. When he got home he connected the spike board to a spare car battery, placed the three balls in position and waited impatiently for the temperatures to reach 60°C. George was quite right, when the red light went out the outsides were still cool. He dropped each ball from five feet and was very pleased with the result. Each one rebounded to almost five feet. He threw a ball at the garage wall and was astonished at the speed with which it came back to him. He took the balls to the top of the garden, where he had an old fishing net slung between two trees, teed them up and, using his driver, hit them into the net. Of course he had no idea how far they would go but there was a splendid crack when they were hit.

That evening, when it was starting to go dark and he was confident that he would meet none of his friends on the course, he went down to the golf club and walked out to the 10th tee. The 10th hole has a wide fairway and there is little chance of losing a golf-ball. He had with him three of the balls previously heated in the car on the way down. He did not think the cores would cool much in the ten minutes it took to walk to the 10th tee. He teed up the first ball and swung back slowly and rhythmically. Then, after a little pause at the top of the backswing, he swung down smoothly and hit the ball. It shot off like a rocket with a most satisfying crack. On and on it went until he lost sight of it in the gloom.

"Wow!" he said aloud, "that was a real humdinger!"

He hit the other two balls with similar results. It was tremendously satisfying. Then he walked down the fairway to collect them. But they'd disappeared! He searched the fairway where they should have been but there was no sign of them. Then he walked to the guide post, 250 yards from the tee, but still they were nowhere to be seen. Where could they have got to? He mustn't lose them! In a panic he hurried back towards the tee and searched desperately on both sides of the fairway. Nothing. His drives had disappeared into thin air. Thoroughly baffled and very upset he walked down the fairway in the dark on his way back to the car. He stumbled over a golf-ball at the bottom of the slope beyond the guide post, 300 yards from the tee. The other two balls were nearby. He was astonished. He picked up the three balls and gazed at them in disbelief. He had just hit three balls over 300 yards against a slight wind. What an achievement! It was unbelievable. It was splendid. Thank you George!

He walked back to the car in a daze and sat motionless in the driver's seat for fully ten minutes before driving home. His plan was succeeding beyond his wildest expectations. From now on every step would have to be thought out carefully, nothing must be left to chance.

The next day Hissin' Syd was completing his round. He'd played well and already won £1. Now they were on the 16th hole playing the bye. He looked across to the first hole and saw Willie Bradley starting out. He hadn't seen Willie for over a week now but they were due to play together in a couple of days. He looked across at Willie with some interest as that worthy individual had a few practice swings on the first tee. He was swinging very quickly, far too quickly, Syd thought. He shook his head slightly. If Willie swung as fast as that his timing would have to be perfect. It wasn't. Willie hit a high ballooning slice that finished in a bunker on the 18th hole. Syd saw him bang the ground with his driver in frustration and then tee up another ball. This time he swung even faster and the ball sliced wildly, whistling over the heads of a four ball on the 18th green. Poor Willie, thought Syd, he really is suffering. If he saw him when they got in he'd have a word and tell him to swing more slowly. The problem was that the old boy thought he knew everything and didn't take kindly to advice. He'd have to be very tactful.

When Syd and his friends were playing the 18th Willie was still on the first hole having searched for his second drive which had finished in the rough by the 18th green. Willie was then about to play an iron shot to the first green. Swinging much too quickly he nearly missed the ball altogether. It travelled about five yards.

"Hard luck," Syd called across, feeling sorry for his adversary. Willie just grunted.

What Syd didn't realise, of course, was that it was all part of the Bradley plan. Before going to the first tee Willie had watched carefully from the clubhouse until he saw Syd on the 15th hole. He knew Syd would watch him. By teeing up the ball on a high tee, playing the ball outside his left foot and closing his eyes, Willie had managed to hit two awful shots. He was pleased, for it is difficult to hit a really bad shot on purpose. He had then waited until he knew Syd would be on the 18th hole before continuing down the first and managing to hit another dreadful shot towards the green. Most satisfactory. He played the second hole very well, out of sight of Syd, for now he was swinging very slowly although not using the special balls. Then he crossed to the ninth hole and played that and the 10th before returning to the clubhouse. He felt very pleased with his golf. It would be difficult to be unpleasant to Syd but he must try.

When Willie walked into the lounge Syd and his partner were in the middle of their toasted tea-cakes. Syd called across and invited Willie to join them. Splendid. Willie sat down and Syd decided the time had come to be helpful. He went about matters with his usual tact.

"You're swinging far too quickly," he said. "It's no wonder you're playing so badly. I've never seen anybody swing so quickly. It's like greased lightning. Not a pretty sight! You'll have to slow down, otherwise you'll just get worse and worse. I'm only trying to be helpful," he added hurriedly, noticing Willie's face getting redder and redder. "I'm looking forward to a good match on Wednesday."

Willie stood up slowly. There was a long pregnant pause. Then he spoke.

"Sydney Sunter", he said, "I was a single figure golfer before you even started the game. I've forgotten more about golf than you'll ever know. I know what you're up to, you're trying your old gamesmanship tricks, but they won't work with me. You're just frightened of me; you know you're in for a real thrashing next Wednesday. You want to try and get your own swing sorted out, never mind mine. I don't mind telling you your swing is dreadful, but it would take years to get it even reasonable, never mind good, and I think you're probably past it now anyway."

There was a shocked silence in the lounge. Everyone was listening. Really, these old boys did take things seriously. Slowly Syd stood up. His face was crimson. He was extremely angry. He spoke slowly, clearly and deliberately,

"Would you care to have a small wager on Wednesday's match," he said, "say £50?"

The tea and toasters gasped. That was going a bit far! It was well known that the club's millionaire liked to play for £5 on the first nine, £5 on the second nine and £5 on the match, but £50 – that really was over the top!

Willie looked long and hard at Syd.

"Make it a straight hundred," he said, to a delighted murmur from the audience, then added offensively, "if you can afford it, that is."

"Right," said Syd. "It will give me great pleasure to take £100 off you and it will serve you jolly well right." And so saying he stormed out of the clubhouse.

It should be said that Willie did feel rather a heel. He had set Syd up beautifully and Syd had fallen for it, hook, line and sinker. But then he remembered how arrogant Syd had become over the past year. He really was a pain in the proverbial. He wasn't a bad chap really, he'd just got a bit above himself and it was necessary to bring him down to earth, then he'd be much more popular and people would enjoy playing with him again. It was for his own good.

The next day Willie again went to the driving range. He concentrated on swinging slowly and smoothly. When he got home he found Sue in a state of considerable agitation. She'd had Jane on the phone.

"What do you think you're doing William?" she asked. "It can't really be true that you're playing Sydney Sunter for £100 tomorrow, can it? Have you gone stark, raving mad?"

"Now calm down dear," said Willie. "It's all part of a plan. I'm doing it for Syd's own good. You know he's become impossible lately. He's so self-opinionated and arrogant that nobody likes him. I thought it would do him a lot of good to find out that he's not really any better than anybody else."

"But you'll never beat him, William," said Sue. "You know you're not playing well. You're just throwing £100 down the drain."

"Sometimes dear," said Willie sanctimoniously, "one has to make sacrifices to help those in need." And he smiled a knowing smile. And Sue, who knew him very well, had a curious feeling that all was not as it seemed and Willie had something up his sleeve. But what? She resolved to watch him very carefully between now and the match. However all he did which was at all unusual was to ask if he could borrow her electrically-powered trolley as he thought it might help him. Of course she said yes but was suspicious, sure that something was afoot.

The match was scheduled to begin at 1.30 in the afternoon. A surprising number of members had turned up to watch. Willie had completed all his preparations. Three Dunlops were already warming up on their spikes, hidden away inside his golf bag. A particularly observant spectator might have noticed two wires emerging from the ball pocket and connected to a second battery – a spare so Willie said to someone who asked. Syd arrived with a caddie and nodded coldly. Willie, on the other hand, was all smiles and good humour.

"Syd," he said, "I'd like to wish you all the best and I've a suggestion to make. I'm quite happy to forget all about the wager if you want, and just play you for £1 as we usually do. It'll give me just as much pleasure to take that off you."

There was a murmur of approval but also disappointment from the gallery. They need not have worried.

"You'll bloody well play me for £100 as we agreed," said Syd, "and I'll bloody well have a great deal of bloody pleasure taking your bloody money!"

The gallery murmured its unqualified approval. That was more like it.

Just then the club champion hurried up with his partner and asked if they might go first as they were playing in the semi-final of the Scratch Cup and would soon be out of the way. Of course Willie and Syd agreed. Big Mike was very popular, with his amiable disposition and huge bulk. His opponent won the toss and went first, hitting a splendid drive 250 yards up the centre of the fairway. Then Big Mike addressed his ball and there was an expectant hush as his huge hands waggled the club head backwards and forwards. Then – wham! – the ball took off like a missile and sped further and further until it eventually came to rest a good 30 yards in front of his opponent's. There was a chorus of gasps and "Good shots!" from the gallery.

"Thank you gentlemen," said Big Mike, "we'll try not to keep you waiting." There were smiles in the crowd. Willie and Syd would never catch up with these two!

Syd won the toss. He addressed his ball and played before Big Mike reached his ball. That was quite usual. Big Mike could hit the ball at least 30 yards further than anyone else. He didn't mind people driving off before he'd played his second shot, in fact he often told people to do so and would have been rather hurt if those behind didn't. Syd's ball landed well short of Big Mike's.

Willie waited until Big Mike had reached his ball, then took Dunlop One from his bag and teed it up.

"I'd better wait till he's out of the way," he said.

"He's been out of the way for the last ten minutes," said Syd scornfully. "There's no way you can get anywhere near him. You stupid bugger," he added under his breath.

But Willie waited until Big Mike had played his second shot, put his club back in his bag and walked on. Then he went. He swung back slowly, paused at the top of the backswing, then swung down with perfect timing. There was a sharp crack as the ball sped away. What a beauty! The ball rose higher and higher as it travelled on and on and on. There was a gasp from those watching. The ball was on the ground now and still running forwards. It passed Big Mike, who stopped in astonishment and gazed back unbelievingly at the tee. When it finally stopped rolling Big Mike bent down to examine the ball, but it was just an ordinary Dunlop. Nobody had ever outdriven him before. Willie's drive had travelled over 300 yards. It was incredible, impossible. But it had happened!

There can be few experiences more satisfying to the senior golfer, especially if he has been losing length lately, than to hit an immense drive when his friends are watching. Willie looked round rather shyly and a little self-consciously. He saw looks of astonishment and disbelief on every face and his heart leapt joyfully. He heard a colourful collection of oaths and exclamations, for golfers can turn a useful phrase when they've a mind to. Syd however didn't say a word, he couldn't, his mouth was open, but try as he might no sound came out. He recovered quickly, however, and muttered a strangled, "Good shot!" before hurrying off up the fairway. But when a golfer finds his best drive is at least 100 yards behind his opponent's it is off-putting and Syd was put off. Completely demoralised he hit his second shot a distance of only 30 yards and his third not much further. His fourth shot was just in front of Willie's drive.

Willie decided to play safe with a five iron. He couldn't possibly reach the green but he could be fairly certain of keeping out of trouble if he played the five iron. When he took the club out of his bag there was a chorus of "Oohs" and "Aahs", and remarks such as, "Who does he think he is, John Daly?" And there was also some merriment. Willie nearly explained that he was only playing safe but decided not to bother and swung the five iron back gently and smoothly. The ball flew away with another satisfying crack and rose high in the air before dropping on the green. And now there was a tremendous roar from the crowd and loud applause. A number of members came up and patted Willie on the back, then they all surged forwards, talking excitedly. Willie was excited too. He'd never before been on the first green in two; it usually took him four. Syd had no chance and, after hitting two more bad shots, picked up his ball and gave Willie the hole.

The second hole is the hardest on the course. The drive needs to be long and straight, and the second shot of pin-point accuracy. A mishit ball invariably finishes in wet boggy ground on the right-hand side of the fairway, leaving the player a difficult shot over trees and bushes onto the green. There was an expectant hush as Willie stood on the tee. If a pin had been dropped the noise would have seemed intolerable. Then loud clapping broke out as the ball was launched at high velocity towards the green. Willie had swung perfectly and his drive carried over 250 yards before bounding on down the fairway. It was a tremendous shot. Willie had never before driven that far at the second hole. The crowd, for crowd it was now as word had got round and many more people had joined the onlookers, applauded enthusiastically. Nobody had seen a drive like that at the second hole. Willie glanced at Syd,

"Hell of a shot!" said Syd weakly. "I don't know …" Then he stopped speaking and gazed intently down the course and Willie saw that his drive had been hit so far he'd actually run out of fairway. As he watched, his ball disappeared over the top of the bank into the long thick grass beyond. Normally, of course, the bank, which was 300 yards from the tee, didn't enter into anybody's calculations, but now, with his tremendous length, Willie was in deep trouble, faced with an almost impossible second shot as the ball would be on a steep downslope in thick rough and he'd have to hack it out somehow, up and over the bushes by the green. He realised that this was almost impossible.

It was clear that Syd thought so too. He aimed well to the left to make sure he didn't go out of bounds and played a safe, steady shot along the fairway. Although it took him two shots before he even reached Willie's drive he was in a good position and, after Willie had hacked vainly at his ball three times, but still not moved it very far, he gave Syd the hole.

Willie walked thoughtfully to the third tee. He was of course delighted with his shots and had enjoyed tremendously the admiration of the members watching. But he now realized that great length can bring its own problems. He would have to view the golf course in an entirely different light and plot a very careful path around it.

When they reached the third tee they met Big Mike and his opponent. By tacit agreement they had decided to wait and let Willie and Syd through. They wanted to see Willie's shots for themselves.

Syd had the honour. Although the third is a par three it is a long one and Syd played his three wood. He hit a good shot which finished on the green. There was a ripple of polite applause but the gallery was really waiting for Willie. What would he play? He usually took his driver but clearly that was out of the question. It would have to be an iron, perhaps a four or five iron.

He glanced at Big Mike and saw that he had a four iron in his hand. But all the trouble was over the green. He'd take his six, he should be all right with that. As he pulled the club from his bag there were cries of, "What are you playing Willie?" And when he showed them the six iron there were gasps and mutters of, "He'll never get there with that!" Even Big Mike shook his head. What did the old boy think he was doing; no-one took a six iron at the third; it was 185 yards.

Willie took the second special ball from his bag and put the first back on its spike to warm up again. There was absolute silence as he teed up and took his stance. He must remember to swing back slowly and smoothly. He did. The ball shot away with that special crack and rose higher and higher as it flew towards the green. A majestic shot. An absolute pearler. The crowd gasped. Willie gasped. Big Mike gasped, then muttered something unrepeatable. Syd's mouth was open so wide a passing bee popped in for a quick look, then flew out again without Syd even noticing. The ball sailed over the green into the small copse of trees beyond. It had been a superb golf shot but again Willie was in trouble. His ball lay directly behind a tree and there was no way he could get onto the green for two. Syd won the hole and was now one up.

The fourth and fifth, however, are long holes, both about 500 yards and fairly straightforward with little serious trouble. Willie reached both greens with a drive and an iron, and won both holes comfortably. One up again. The sixth is a difficult par four – a dog-leg to the left around a field, with an old oak tree in the corner of the dog-leg. The best line is up to the right leaving a long second to the green. Many years ago Henry Cotton, in his prime, had visited the club and, at that hole, had hit his tee shot over the oak tree, nearly reaching the green. But that was a long time ago and the oak tree was now much bigger. Today nobody ever tried to clear it and Willie certainly didn't intend to. The crowd didn't expect him to either. No-one went that way. But whilst Willie's back swing was smooth and slow he had become over-confident as one does when hitting the ball well and, turning too soon at the top of his swing, he swung down too quickly and the result was a tremendous hook. But this was no ordinary hook. The ball started off straight but moved further and further left as it rose higher and higher until it sailed effortlessly over the big oak tree, finishing close to the green.

A splendid shot. From that position Willie could use his putter. There was a great roar from the crowd and Willie smiled rather deprecatingly as he turned to Syd.

"Didn't get it quite right," he said, "but it's finished OK."

It was of course inevitable that Syd would top his shot into the ditch in front of the tee. He picked out and played on manfully but it took him three more shots to reach the green and Willie easily won the hole.

"Took your advice," he said to Syd at the next tee, "I'm swinging more slowly. You should try it sometime."

Syd glared balefully at him.

"You're only two up," he hissed. "You haven't won yet."

And indeed Willie lost the next hole and, more importantly, one of his precious balls in the river behind the green. The seventh is only a short par three but Willie simply had no idea what club to play. Normally he would have used a five iron, as Syd did, but today he took a nine iron and the ball bounced once on the back of the green, then shot off into the river beyond. Willie was not unduly worried. He still had two special balls left although it did mean that he would have to plan matters fairly carefully as it took about half-an-hour for a ball to warm up after it had been used. At the eighth hole, a long par three onto an elevated green, Willie played a superb seven iron but then took four putts on the difficult sloping green. However softly he tried to hit his putts the ball came off the putter so quickly it always went too far. He went backwards and forwards from one side of the hole to the other and eventually was quite lucky to get down in five and halve the hole with Syd. He walked very pensively to the ninth tee. So far he'd had very little putting to do as the holes had mostly been won or lost before they'd reached the greens. It was clear that putting was going to be a problem.

At the ninth hole, much to the delight of the crowd, Willie hit another monster drive and needed only a six iron to reach the green on this par five. Syd also played the hole well but was on the green in three strokes so that if Willie could get down in two putts he would win the hole and be two in front at the turn. After his experience on the eighth green he was determined to hit his first putt gently and this he did – far too gently in fact, for the ball stopped a good 10 feet from the hole. Syd putted up quite dead, so Willie had to sink his next putt to win the hole. He looked at the line carefully and then gave the ball a firm rap. It shot off the putter head like an express train, fortunately in the right direction. The ball hit the back of the hole, jumped at least six inches in the air and – what a relief! – dropped back in the hole. Two up at the turn.

The 10th was halved in eight. Willie was over the green in two but misjudged his chip back so that it sailed back over the green again. Trying to hit the fourth too gently he went into the bunker. Trying to hit the fifth too gently he stayed in the bunker. His sixth was out, on the green, and he managed to get down in two putts to halve with Syd, who had spent most of the hole in the trees.

But then Syd seemed to get a new lease of life. He holed a good putt for a winning two at the 11th and his perfect par four at the 12th was good enough to beat Willie, who was over the green in two and fluffed his little chip. Back to all square; back to where they started with everything still to play for! Those watching had now realised that the match could go either way and many were the side bets negotiated and re-negotiated.

The short 13th was played in an atmosphere of great tension. Both put their tee shots on the green, Syd with a four iron, Willie with a nine. Syd putted up well short. Willie was well past. Syd holed his and then, with great courage, so did Willie. The crowd applauded. The players deserved it. On the 14th tee Willie realised with a shock that he had been playing with the same special ball since the 10th hole. He usually changed the balls every three holes but had forgotten to do so in the excitement of the match. He hurriedly put ball number two back on its heating spike and took out ball number three. It felt very hot and he dropped it involuntarily to avoid burning his fingers. He kicked it towards the next tee but when he placed it on the tee peg, the plastic tee softened and the ball fell off onto the ground.

"Good God Willie," exclaimed Syd, "what's happened to that tee?"

"Oh, nothing Sydney," said Willie, "it's been in my bag a long time. They do go all crumbly you know. Things just don't last like they used to. It's this plastic rubbish."

"It looks to me as if it's melted," said Syd suspiciously.

"Melted?" said Willie. "Don't be ridiculous, how could it?"

He quickly bent down and teed the ball on a wooden tee, picking up what remained of the plastic tee and throwing it into the bushes.

Willie addressed the ball and swung the club back slowly and smoothly. He paused at the top of his swing and swung the club down, once again with perfect timing. When the club head hit the ball there was an almighty bang and the ball disintegrated, small pieces flying everywhere. The crowd gasped and some members ran forward to look for the pieces. Fortunately for Willie these were very small indeed.

"I've never seen that happen before," said Syd sceptically. "I reckon there's something funny about that ball!"

"No-one's ever hit 'em as hard before," someone called out from the crowd. "Don't be such a bad sport!"

"Me!" said Syd. "I'm not a bad sport. I'm not suggesting anything. I just think it's very odd, that's all. I've seen balls break into two or three pieces but never so many and with such a bang. Has anybody else?"
There was much muttering and many heads shaken.

"You'll have to play another Willie," someone called out. "There's no penalty."

Willie had been maintaining a dignified silence whilst all this was going on. When Syd had commented on the curious destruction of his golf-ball he had assumed what he felt was a suitable expression of deep hurt and sorrow such as any sportsman would have put on, and accompanied it with a sharp intake of breath. But he realized the grave position he was now in. He only had one more special ball and that wouldn't be ready for half-an-hour at least That meant he'd have to play the next three holes with an ordinary ball. An ordinary ball! The thought sent a shock wave of horror through him. He'd come to rely on his special balls, without them he felt – well – he felt helpless! It was awful. He felt the first stirrings of panic. There were all these people watching and they'd see him play his normal shots. He'd be lucky to reach the bunker which was only about 170 yards from the tee. And they were all expecting him to carry the ditch 250 yards away!

With trembling hands Willie fumbled in his bag for another ball and, with some difficulty, teed it up. There was an expectant silence from the crowd as they looked forward to another monster drive. Willie swung back slowly and gracefully but, in his anxiety, swung down far too quickly. The shot was sliced badly and the ball finished deep in the rough on the right of the fairway, only 50 yards from the tee. There was a stunned silence from the crowd and then someone called out,

"What's up Willie, have you forgotten how to hit 'em?"

"He doesn't want to smash up any more balls," someone else said and there was a ripple of laughter.

Syd played a good shot down the fairway and together they set off to look for Willie's ball.

"Not quite up to your usual standard Willie," said Syd. "It didn't go off with the same noise as the other shots either. It was extraordinary what happened to that other ball. Where did you get it by the way? Did you buy it from our Pro?"

"I can't remember," said Willie. "I've had it a long time. Those balls were presents I think. I've got another somewhere," he added as an afterthought.

"I'd like to see it," said Syd, far too eagerly for Willie's liking.

"I'll see if I can find it," said Willie.

Fortunately they had now reached the rough where Willie's ball lay, which had already been found by one of the spectators. Willie was relieved to see that it was lying badly. No-one could get far from a lie like that. He hit it as hard as he could with his nine iron. It came out well and plugged into the face of a fairway bunker. Again it was in a dreadful place. Gary Player would have found it difficult to get out from there. The crowd however had no doubts of Willie's ability. They were confident that, not only would he get the ball out of the bunker, but would also put it on the green 160 yards away. There were murmurs of encouragement as they looked forward to another Herculean feat.

"You watch. He'll probably carry it all the way to the green and drop it like a grasshopper with sore feet by the hole."

"There'll be a bloody crater in that bunker when he's dug that one out."
Such were the comments heard by Willie as he viewed the situation with some dismay.

The spectators surrounded the bunker and waited expectantly. Willie knew that time was of the essence. Somehow he had to delay matters as long as possible so that his one remaining Dunlop would have time to heat up. He walked forwards towards the green as all the pros do on TV.

"Told you," someone said in the crowd. "He's looking at where the pin is. He'll drop this right on the flag, you mark my words."

As he walked slowly back to the bunker Willie had a brainwave. A plan was forming in his mind. As if by magic his gloom lifted. He knew what he would do. He would use the well tried and tested techniques of gamesmanship. If he played his cards right he should be able to delay matters sufficiently so that the special ball would be ready for the 16th tee. Yes, Potter's Medical Ploy would fit the bill perfectly! He would probably lose the 14th and 15th holes but he'd only be two down and felt sure he could win the last three holes and the match if, that is, the Dunlop was at optimum temperature.

There was a new spring in his step as he walked into the bunker. He smiled confidently at the spectators. He addressed what he could see of the ball buried deep in the soft sand and had several dummy swings à la Faldo. Then he tightened his grip, shut his eyes, swung back as far as he possibly could and hit the sand well behind the ball with tremendous force. There was sand everywhere – in his hair, in his mouth, up his nose. With a sharp cry he stumbled out of the bunker, both hands over his eyes.

"Got sand in your eyes Willie?" enquired Syd sympathetically, for his opponent was clearly in great pain, groaning pitifully and rubbing his eyes.

"Just give me a minute," said Willie bravely, between groans. "Can't see a thing just at the moment. Did I get out?"

"Ball came out like a rocket," said Syd. "Bloody marvellous shot. It's nearly on the green. Blink as much as you can, that usually helps. And don't rub your eyes," he added wisely.

Willie peeped through his fingers and saw, to his astonishment, that his ball was, in fact, over the ditch and nearly on the green. That was a bonus! But he must delay matters a bit longer yet. Fortunately he hadn't got any sand in his eyes so he could rub them to make them red. He asked the members nearby if anyone had a clean handkerchief and could help to get the grit out of his eyes. Heroically he endured, with only a few sharp intakes of breath, the clumsy poking of a well-meaning surgeon (who was a member) before announcing that his eyes felt much better and he was almost ready to proceed.

"Don't hurry," said Syd, "I want to beat you fair and square!"

"I'll be all right now," said Willie stoutly. "I'm afraid I've held everything up," he continued as he walked very slowly down the fairway to loud applause from the crowd.

Meanwhile Syd played short of the ditch for two and then onto the green in three. Willie, using his putter from off the green, then managed to get down in two putts to halve the hole in five. Still all square, but now the long 15th stretched endlessly ahead and, after hitting a normal tee shot of about 170 yards to the great disappointment of the spectators, Willie knew he'd have to resort to what senior gamesmen will recognise as Stephen Potter's Most Famous Medical Ploy. He played his second, a reasonable enough shot but not what the crowd expected at all, then waited whilst Syd played. Syd hit a magnificent shot which finished well in front of Willie's and nearly on the green. Then Willie stood, head bowed, motionless, whilst everyone else moved forward.

"What's the matter now Willie?" called out Syd, growing impatient.

"Sorry," said Willie faintly.

"What did you say?" asked Syd in exasperation.

"Sorry," said Willie again, even more faintly. "Sorry, sorry, sorry. Damn!" The gallery had stopped now and a few walked back to Willie, as did Syd.

"Are you OK," enquired Syd rather more kindly. After all, if Willie were to have a coronary then he, Syd, would naturally be able to claim the match. Such things inevitably spring to mind at times like this.

"It's nothing," said Willie, breathing in what he felt were appropriate short gasps, "just a little heart thing. It comes on if I hit the ball too hard. I felt it on the last hole but didn't want to say anything. Don't worry, it'll pass. The doc told me ... told me I'd only got a short ..." His voice died away with a deathly sort of rattle and the spectators pressed forward, enthralled. Was this the end of Willie Bradley? What a man! To continue playing and battling on so manfully when he had only a short ... well, presumably only a short time to live! What courage! What sportsmanship! What drama!

Willie noticed the little red light on his trolley had gone off, indicating that the last of his special balls was now up to temperature. Now was the time to stage a recovery, but it must be gradual. He straightened up slowly and looked around, like a man awakening from a long sleep. When he spoke it was in a voice heavy with emotion and relief.

"Thank goodness," he said, "that's better. It's passed off. Good. I'm fine now. Let's get on with it, shall we. No point in hanging around. Mustn't let these little medical problems get in the way." And so saying he marched briskly off to a spontaneous burst of applause from the crowd. However, as one member said to another, he was obviously putting a brave face on things and clearly wasn't himself yet for he hit a very bad third into a dreadful spot in the bunker and, when Syd's third shot finished quite near the pin, Willie picked up his ball, conceding the hole. He knew he would lose it anyway, so he may as well do so and gain a bit more sympathy from the crowd whilst he was about it. It was inevitable that Syd would feel bad about winning a hole in such circumstances. Indeed some of those watching commented that it would be sensible to abandon the match and call it all square before anyone died, but Willie wouldn't hear of it, saying he would be quite all right now.

It had upset Syd though, for he hit a very weak drive at the fairly short, par four 16th. Willie teed up the hot ball. It was amazing the confidence it gave him. He had a slow and smooth practice swing. The crowd were quiet now, fascinated. Could he recapture his old power and, if so, would the effort be the end of him? Willie hit his drive. There was the old familiar crack as the ball flew away, remaining airborne for what seemed an eternity before dropping onto the green 337 yards distant. There was thunderous applause and a buzz of excited chatter. No-one could remember that green being driven before! Ever!

"Are you OK Willie?" asked someone anxiously in the crowd.

"Fine thanks," said Willie. "I held back on it as I knew I didn't need to hit it too hard."

"Wow," said the member. "Where'd it have gone if he'd really hit it?" he enquired of no-one in particular.

Willie won the hole easily, for Syd was completely demoralised and conceded the hole after taking three more shots to reach the green. All square again, two to play. The 17th, a short par three, is a tricky hole, with a big bunker on the right and a steep slope beyond the green falling away into rough grass. Willie usually played his three wood but was so anxious not to go too far that, to the delight of the crowd, he took out his sand wedge. However he miss-hit the shot and the ball finished in a little pot bunker short of the green. Fortunately Syd didn't do much better and the hole was eventually halved in five, after much toing and froing and looking at lines on the green.

They had now reached the last hole all square. Both were exhausted. Willie had the honour. The 18th hole is a gentle dog-leg to the left around a line of conifers marking the boundary of the course. In the old days you could, if you dared, go over these trees and finish close to the green, but now they were too tall and you must play safely to the right leaving perhaps a seven iron to the green. Willie looked at the trees. It would be the ultimate test if he could clear them, but if he pulled his shot the consequences would be too awful to contemplate. He would be out of bounds in the lane running alongside the course and would almost certainly lose the match and £100. The crowd waited expectantly. "Go on Willie, you can do it," someone called out. "Give it a go!" Willie saw money changing hands as bets were laid and realised he had no choice, he had to go for it!

There was a hush as he lined up on the third tree from the right. The atmosphere was electric. Willie took a deep breath and swung his driver back in one graceful, rhythmical movement. "Slow back, slow down and hit into the follow through," he could remember his father telling him as if it were yesterday. There was a crack as the ball sped jet-propelled up and up and over the third tree from the right. It was a perfect shot, a tremendous drive and must be nearly on the green. A great roar went up from the crowd and then loud applause. Willie felt great. He looked at Syd who was staring open-mouthed down the fairway and felt a twinge of remorse. Syd had played so well and behaved impeccably although the effect of Willie's shots must have been shattering.

Syd's drive went safely down the fairway and they walked together towards his ball.

"I would like to say Willie," said Syd, "that I have never seen anyone hit the ball as well as you've done this afternoon. I take back all I said after our last game. It has been a privilege to play with you and, whatever the outcome of this match, I congratulate you on your play. It has been magnificent. I hope we can have another game sometime when there aren't so many people around."

Willie was touched. He stopped and put out his hand, "I would be delighted," he said and they shook hands warmly.

When they reached Syd's ball the green was in sight and Willie's ball was only ten yards from the hole.

"Well, I think you've beaten me you old bugger," said Syd, "unless I can get this dead." With great courage he played an excellent shot which finished in the centre of the green. It would be Willie to putt first. The crowd applauded loudly.

"Well done Syd," said Willie, "super shot."

When they reached the green Willie putted and his ball finished very close to the hole. Syd walked forward and picked it up, conceding the three. Syd had to hole his putt now to halve the match. It was a difficult putt of perhaps 20 feet and he would have to allow for a lot of borrow. If he missed it he would lose £100. Again there was utter silence. Syd looked at the line of his putt from every angle and then, when he could put it off no longer, addressed his ball and prepared to play.

As Willie watched he found, to his surprise, that he was hoping that Syd would hole his putt. After all he'd proved his point and shown them all how far he could hit the ball, albeit with a bit of help. And Syd had behaved so well. He wasn't such a bad chap after all and it would be nice to play with him again. Suddenly Willie knew what to do.

"Stop!" he called out, "I'll give you that one. It would be a shame for anyone to lose this match."

He walked forward and picked up Syd's ball and the two old friends shook hands. The crowd clapped enthusiastically and more than one of those present recalled a similar incident at Royal Birkdale in 1969, when the outcome of the Ryder Cup depended on the last putt on the last green in the last match between two very great players. Then too, much was at stake.

WINDY CONDITIONS

... or how to nobble the ladies' president.

There were very few people Willie Bradley disliked. It wasn't in his nature. He was affable, easy-going and had many friends. But Hilary Bottomley, president of the ladies' section of the Black Hills Golf Club, was someone he really, really disliked. Not only was she an out-and-out snob and very arrogant, but it was she who had blocked the application to join the club of Willie's sister-in-law who had returned to the UK after a long spell abroad. No-one had dreamt that Sue's sister would not get in, especially as Sue was a past president herself and highly respected. But Hilary had pointed out that the ladies' section was full and, anyway, they were looking for younger, low-handicap members, not elderly ladies with high handicaps. And the trouble was that the ladies' president, by tradition, always had the final say in such matters.

To make things worse, Willie and Sue had, against all odds, reached the final of the mixed foursomes' Challenge Trophy and their opponents were none other than Hilary and her partner Desmond Duxbury. Willie had nothing against Desmond, he quite liked him, but Hilary should have been playing with her husband Bill.

When the trophy had been donated, years and years ago, the idea was that, if at all possible, husbands and wives should play together, thereby strengthening relationships and promoting good fellowship between families in the club. But Hilary knew very well that if husband Bill had been her partner she would have lost in the first round, whereas with Desmond, a former county player, she had reached the final in their first season together and they were almost certain to win. Bill had been very good about it when she suggested she might play with Desmond. In fact he'd encouraged her to do so, saying he was quite happy to stay in the bar whilst the matches took place.

For his part Desmond had been flattered when the ladies' president had invited him to partner her. He had been a member for only five years and was naturally still viewed with suspicion. He felt the invitation signalled a measure of acceptance by the hierarchy. However, after playing four rounds with Hilary he realised how dearly he was paying for the privilege. She was so bossy and unkind, and did not treat their opponents with any respect. She was undoubtedly a magnificent golfer but he resolved that, next year, even if they were the defending champions, he would be unavailable.

And so it was that, a few weeks before the final, Willie sat in his favourite armchair, sipping his favourite single malt and wondering how on earth he and Sue could beat Hilary and Desmond. When he was younger Willie had been a low handicap golfer but now, in his 75th year, he was much plumper and his handicap was 22. Sue had never been a good golfer; she was too small and chatty. She played for pleasure and was popular with everyone. Even though he could, when in the mood, raise his game to beat many opponents, Willie knew that on this occasion in a mixed foursome with Sue, he could not possibly do enough and they were sure to get beaten.

He reflected on how lucky they had been to reach the final. In the first round they had been drawn against two absolute beginners who often missed the ball altogether, and it had been impossible to lose. They had been given the next match when the male member of the opposition had disappeared from the district taking with him the wife of another member. Willie and Sue actually won the third round on one of those happy days when everything went right and there the story should have ended as their opponents in the semi-final were a popular husband and wife team who had won the cup the previous year and, so far, had swept aside all opponents this year. But, as luck would have it, a burst appendix meant another walk-over and so, to their and everyone else's surprise and delight, the Bradleys were in the final and, although they couldn't win, that in itself was, for them, a great achievement.

So, as Willie sat and sipped his Highland Park, all of a sudden a most outrageous, disgraceful and appalling idea came into his head. Was it possible? It just might be ... and it would certainly throw Hilary off-balance. It was ingenious and he felt sure he could make it work. He couldn't help smiling as he thought of the effect it would have on Hilary. She'd be devastated – totally embarrassed and humiliated. Surely it would put her off her game. He and Sue would then have a chance of winning and certainly they'd have no chance whatsoever otherwise.

It would have been different if he'd liked Hilary. He liked most people. But she was such a very difficult person to like. Sue had told him that when past presidents of the ladies' section got together to discuss whom to invite to be the next vice-president, there had been many misgivings when the name of Hilary Bottomley came up once again. Nobody really wanted her but the problem was that it was her turn and, in fact, had been for many years. However previous committees had always found some excuse for not inviting her.

Then, two years ago, the nettle had finally been grasped and now that Hilary was ladies' president she was proving to be as unpopular as predicted. She'd accepted immediately when asked, pointing out that her mother had been president of the ladies' section when she'd been much younger. She couldn't imagine why she hadn't been asked before but looked forward to making many changes – a remark calculated to upset most of the ladies who preferred everything to remain exactly as it always had been.

That night Willie tossed and turned in bed with so many thoughts racing round in his brain that sleep was quite impossible. He kept coming back to the final and his idea. It wouldn't guarantee their success of course, even if everything went according to plan. And, if it didn't, what a fuss there would be. He'd have a lot of explaining to do. He might even have to resign from the club. He mustn't say anything to Sue whatever he decided. She wouldn't approve and, even more importantly, if she knew what was going on she wouldn't be able to behave normally. He'd have to keep it to himself. It would be a real challenge to make it work but it would be fun.

It wasn't until daybreak that Willie finally decided that he would try to put his idea into practice. He squared his conscience with the thought that he wasn't really doing it for himself but for Sue, because she'd been so humiliated by that business with her sister's application and it would please her more than anything to beat Hilary in the final. It was gamesmanship of course but in this case he felt it could be justified. Now that the fateful decision had been made Willie Bradley, retired engineer and inventor extraordinary, fell fast asleep.

Next morning he was up bright and early and disappeared into his study immediately after breakfast There he sat in his old armchair and began to make lists of what was required, every now and then breaking off to draw little diagrams to illustrate possible ways of carrying out his ideas. Willie was designing a remote-controlled farting machine. He intended to attach it to Hilary's trolley. It would not be visible and, at carefully chosen moments, he would make it fart realistically. Perhaps when Hilary was walking with the trolley close to her, or even when the trolley was near to Hilary on a tee and she was actually taking her swing, he would organise it so that the sound was projected away from the trolley and towards Hilary. Then everyone would think she was responsible and she would be totally embarrassed. Hopefully her game would be ruined. Willie felt sure he could devise something capable of emitting a whole range of different farts – small subdued squeaks, low rumbles, loud booms, or even – and he couldn't help smiling as he thought of the ladies' president – even a disgusting wet splutter of a fart; that would surely destroy her. He thought it might also be possible to incorporate an odour too, and the ability to accompany the sound with an appalling smell would certainly add to the realism. But that would be difficult. He'd have to give it more thought.

Willie had a small workshop at the back of the garage where all the development work took place. He experimented with infra-red remote controllers and solenoids powered by Duracell batteries. He built an electronic device which squeaked beautifully. For a time he struggled with the problem of producing the deeper notes he felt to be essential for someone of Hilary's build. Eventually, with great ingenuity, he employed an old motor horn to produce a loud realistic honk. However his greatest achievement was the balloon, inflated and held with its neck gripped within a small tube of water. When Willie activated a valve, air was released vigorously through the water making a splendid, spluttering, gurgling noise. He found that if he incorporated a small cylinder of compressed gas from an old soda siphon, he could blow the balloon up again so that it had the capacity to emit at least five more farts of considerable power.

It might be said that things got a little out of hand then , for Willie became so interested in the technical beauty of his invention that he continued until he had perfected a control mechanism that allowed him to switch from one sound to another, then produce, if he so wished, a sequence of farts starting soft and low, then ending with a blockbuster of awesome power. He could also add overtones such as the wet splutter, the squeak, or the staccato rip-rap in which the fart was fired off in a stuttering sequence of pops.

Most of his work took place when he knew Sue would be out. But on one occasion she arrived home early and heard the strangest sounds coming from the garage as soon as she climbed out of her car which, very luckily, she had parked on the drive. She hurried inside to find Willie in his workshop with five inflated balloons held in a rack over a water bath. He was releasing the air at different rates using the remote controller from the TV set There was a curious, most unpleasant odour that made her wrinkle her nose in disgust.

"For Heaven's sake William," she said, "What are you doing? That dreadful noise can be heard next door. And what is that awful smell?"

Willie smiled, pleased.

"Can it really dear?" he said. "That is good. I'll open a window. I think we've had cats in here."

But he stopped work immediately and quickly ushered her out, for he did not want her to recall those sounds or that smell.

When he was satisfied that he could produce realistic sounds, Willie addressed the problem of concealing the various components of his device on a golf trolley. After a great deal of thought he decided his best chance was in one of the wheels. Fortunately Hilary used an electric trolley which had relatively large side wheels. Willie bought a spare wheel and examined it carefully. The tyre was solid rubber but could be detached from the rim. Using a scalpel he carefully cut a number of holes in the inside surface. One hole had to be for the motor horn; another, rectangular, was to hold the box containing the collection of little pipes used to produce the different sounds. On the opposite side two holes were cut, one for the sausage-shaped balloon, the other for the tube of water necessary for the gurgles and splutters. The parts were connected together by plastic tubes.

He assembled all the bits together and tried out his invention in the garage. It worked well but it was more difficult than he expected to achieve the necessary degree of control. However, he practised hard and before long was able to produce a great variety of eminently satisfying farts, some of which even surprised him with their realism.

The night before the final Willie told Sue he was going to take the dog down to the playing fields to give her a good run. On his way home he drove to the golf club. It was quite dark but he had a torch. The golf trolleys were all kept in a locked room beneath the professional's shop. He dare not put on any lights for fear that someone would come to investigate, but soon found Hilary's trolley in its usual spot and, using his torch and the tools he'd brought, was able to replace her trolley wheel with the special one. The wheel looked rather new so he rubbed it with soil until it was indistinguishable from all the others.

The day of the final dawned bright and clear. Sue was clearly nervous for she talked even more than usual. She hoped desperately that she wouldn't make a fool of herself in front of the spectators. There was always a small gallery for the final of the mixed foursomes knock-out and Sue knew that the ladies' vice-president and the ladies' captain would feel honour-bound to attend. Several other members of the ladies' committee would be there too. Willie did his best to calm her down, pointing out that they had been very lucky to reach the final and it didn't matter now what happened. They weren't expected to win against Hilary and Desmond even though they would receive strokes at every hole except the 17th.

Predictably, Hilary and Desmond began in impressive fashion. A perfect par five at the first hole was quite good enough to beat Willie and Sue who had started nervously and finally holed out in seven. The second hole is probably the hardest on the course requiring, as it does, a long second to a closely guarded green. The out-of-bounds fence runs all the way down the right-hand side. Hilary drove long and straight, then Desmond played a beautiful two iron over the marshy ground on the right, drawing the ball back onto the green to finish only five feet from the hole. The onlookers applauded. Willie and Sue got into all sorts of trouble, eventually picking their ball up when they'd had six and were still in the bunker. Two down already and it was clear that the match would soon be over. Hilary had a smug, self-satisfied look as she marched briskly off to the third tee. Sue, on the other hand, looked very dejected. She felt as if she could do nothing right. She was so nervous and so sorry for letting William down. She knew she was swinging far too quickly, because she was so anxious, but she didn't seem to be able to do anything about it. The harder she tried, the worse she became.

The third hole is a long par three, with a ditch on the right of the fairway and bunkers guarding both sides of the narrow entrance to the green. Desmond, with the honour, played first – a good four iron shot but pulled slightly. The ball finished short of the left-hand bunker, leaving Hilary with a straightforward chip from a good lie onto the green. Willie was not so fortunate. He had needed his driver and, although the ball started off well enough heading straight for the entrance to the green, the shot was sliced and the ball came to rest short of the bunker on the right, lying on the path to the next tee. Sue would have to play a delicate, high shot over the bunker from bare ground – a horrid prospect!

"Sorry dear," said Willie, who fully appreciated the difficulty of the situation.

"Not to worry," replied Sue, smiling at him without a hint of criticism. She knew he'd done his best.

Nonetheless she was worried. She knew that if she kept her head down and made a long, slow swing with her wedge, all would be well. The ball would float up, over the bunker, and plop down softly onto the green. Then they would get a four and probably halve the hole with Hilary and Desmond. On the other hand, if she lifted her head and fluffed the shot, the ball would finish in the bunker or, if she thinned the shot, the ball would skim over the green into the trees beyond. She must remember not to grip the club too tightly, to relax, keep her head down, think positively and picture the ball on the green and not in the bunker. Oh dear, there were so many things to remember and all these people were watching her. She desperately hoped she wouldn't make an absolute fool of herself as it looked as if she'd have to play first.

Sue took her sand wedge from her bag, had a nervous little practice swing and then played a good shot from the very difficult lie. Unfortunately the ball just failed to clear the bunker, catching the top lip and rolling back into the sand. There was a chorus of disappointed "Oohs" and "Hard lucks" from the gallery.

"Good shot dear," said Willie, "you did very well. It was an awful position and you nearly made it."

Hilary, however, would have none of it.

"You'd never have fluffed that one in your younger days Sue," she called out unkindly. "You didn't have a full enough swing and your right hand action was very weak. Come over here and watch me."

Hilary then played a perfect shot from a much easier position. The ball finished two feet from the hole. There was a muted ripple of applause from the gallery. She was, after all, the ladies' president and it had been a very good shot. What a pity she was so obnoxious.

"There," said Hilary, "I told you these shots are easy."

"Good shot Hilary," said Sue without moving her lips, her features set in a fixed smile. "I wish you'd fall and break your silly neck," she added under her breath so that only Willie could hear.

Although Willie played out well from the bunker the ball did not go in the hole and they went three down.

"That woman says the stupidest things," said Sue to Willie as they walked to the next tee. "I wish we could somehow win this next hole."

"We might," said Willie. "We just might."

When they reached the next tee Willie walked round the tee and casually moved Hilary's trolley until it was opposite the ball she had teed up. The trolley wheels were pointing in her direction. Hilary was having several practice swings. Willie felt in his pocket for the infra-red controller.

There was silence as the ladies' president addressed her ball. She swung back slowly, eventually reaching a perfect position at the top of the backswing, club horizontal, left arm straight, right elbow tucked into her side. And then she farted – not loudly but quite distinctly. It was one of those farts which the farter hopes will pass unnoticed, although, in his heart of hearts, he knows it will not. It was a subdued, demure, lady-like fart and those standing by the tee couldn't help smiling briefly, though naturally they appeared to have heard nothing. But Hilary was put off her stroke and topped the ball, which trickled into the ditch in front of the tee. She looked around angrily, for she knew she hadn't been responsible for that unfortunate noise but, to her surprise, there was nobody behind her and she frowned in bewilderment as she picked up her tee and stood to one side to allow Sue to play. She kept glancing around but no-one was near her. Now that she was not the centre of attention Sue had no difficulty in hitting a splendid shot down the middle of the fairway.

After Hilary and Desmond had picked out of the ditch under penalty of one stroke, they played the rest of the hole well but could not retrieve the situation. Their opponents got a five nett four and won the hole.

On the long fifth Willie and Sue reached the green in five whilst Hilary had to play their fourth shot from behind the bunker by the side of the green. It was quite an easy shot really, the ball sitting up nicely and plenty of green to work with. There was little doubt that the ball would finish close to the hole.

As Willie walked past Hilary's trolley he happened to bump into it so that the wheels pointed at Hilary as she crouched over her ball, a picture of concentration. She was supremely confident, being an excellent wedge player, and she knew she could chip the ball near the hole. She visualised the shot, noting where the ball should land so that it would run down the little slope and on towards the hole. She wished that fool, her vice-president, would stop talking for a minute. She ought to be watching Hilary, not talking. She'd tell her about it after she'd played this shot.

She glanced once more towards the hole – and farted. This time quite loudly. It was a high pressure squeak heard by everyone. Hilary couldn't understand it. She knew she hadn't farted but no-one was near her. She straightened up and looked round. Where had the noise come from? Intrigued, the gallery were gazing at her in happy amazement. What a splendid thing to happen to Hilary, poor dear. How embarrassing! Now there was total silence. Even the ladies' vice-president had stopped talking. Hilary addressed the ball once more. As she drew the club back she farted again ... and again ... and again, each one lasting longer than its predecessor. The final fart was a beauty, a long drawn-out splutter that bubbled on and on. Someone in the gallery applauded.
"By Jove Hilary, that's better out than in," said Desmond, bravely taking the bull by the horns and trying to laugh off the whole embarrassing episode.
"Don't be a fool," said Hilary furiously. "It was not I!"

Even in that moment of extreme stress her grammar was perfect. She was, after all, a Cheltenham girl. She spoke with such conviction that many of those watching looked round to see if anyone else could possibly be responsible. But there was no-one near her and they were forced to the conclusion, first that it was Hilary, and second that she wanted to pretend it wasn't. In consequence, mostly being well-bred members of the golf club, those watching decided that whatever else occurred they must act as if nothing had happened. Little did they realise how difficult that would be.

Once more Hilary addressed the ball. She swung the club back a little way, tentatively, and waited. Nothing happened. She started again and this time got to the top of her backswing, and waited. Absolute silence. The gallery held its breath. She addressed the ball for the third time. Determined to play the shot she swung back quickly, far too quickly, and stabbed nervously at the ball which disappeared rapidly into the greenside bunker. Willie smiled. He'd calculated correctly that, after the shock she'd had, not even Hilary would have been able to play that delicate little chip shot onto the green. He hadn't had to interfere at all. When Desmond failed to get out of the bunker Hilary picked up their ball and marched off to the next tee without a word, desperate to leave that humiliating hole.

Only one down now and, with another stroke to come at the sixth, Sue hit a beautiful drive to loud applause. Then, when Willie somehow got his shot on the green, applause could be heard all over the course. Willie and Sue won the hole without needing their stroke. Now that the match was all square Willie decided not to do anything for a while, waiting to see how the match progressed. It was clear that Hilary was nervous and ill at ease, totally baffled by what had happened and uncertain whether anything else would occur. Her swing was tentative, her shots lacked authority, her confidence had been shattered. Sue, on the other hand, was playing magnificently. Conscious that she was not the one being watched with such interest by the gallery, she was able to relax and swing easily. The match swung one way, then the other. After 13 holes they were still all square. Hilary was beginning to play more assertively now, regaining much of her old confidence and arrogance.

On the 14th hole Willie and Sue had a stroke but were in the greenside bunker for three whilst Hilary and Desmond were on the green in three, although a long way from the hole. It was Willie's shot. He was uncertain whether he could even get the ball out of the bunker for it was plugged in the face. He shuffled his feet in the best Gary Player fashion, took a full backswing and hit the sand two inches behind the ball. The ball came out perfectly and stopped on the very edge of the hole. They would get a five, nett four. Desmond would have to hole his putt for a half! The gallery applauded loudly and Willie, pleased, took his cap off and bowed in all directions.

"Well done William," said Sue. "Brilliant! I don't know how you do it." And then, quite without thinking, she walked up to their ball as it lay by the side of the hole and picked it up. After all it was stone dead.

"Sue!" said Willie, aghast.

"That's OK," said Desmond. "We'll give you that."

"We will not," said Hilary. "You picked your ball up so it's our hole. I'm sorry, but rules are rules. You've lost the hole. You should know better."

"I say Hilary," said Desmond, "it's not that serious. I think we should give them the five. They deserve it after that bunker shot of Willie's."

There was a murmur of approval from the gallery but Hilary had picked up their ball and was already on her way to the 15th tee, secure in the knowledge that the match was being played strictly according to the rules of the game, if not the spirit. There was a loud buzz of chatter as the unfortunate situation was discussed. Hilary was right of course, but who else would have claimed the hole like that.

"Oh William," said Sue. "I'm so sorry. How stupid of me. It was such a lovely shot you played in that bunker."

"Don't worry," said Willie, and there was something in his tone that made her glance at him in surprise. "Don't worry," he repeated, "I'll take care of everything."

The 15th is the last par five on the course, a long hole in the shape of a dog-leg bending round to the right. The ground falls away on the right-hand side and balls hit on that side of the fairway run away leaving difficult shots to the green. The men were driving from the tee and they both hit splendid drives, with Desmond's ball, as usual, 50 yards in front of Willie's.

As the ladies walked up the fairway it was noticeable that, whereas Sue was surrounded by many members, consoling and encouraging her, Hilary, the ladies' president, walked alone, aloof and haughty. Even her vice-president did not feel inclined to accompany her. It was just what Willie wanted.

There was complete silence as Sue lined up to play the second shot and then loud applause as the ball, hit perfectly, ran on and on towards the far distant green.

"Well done Sue," said Willie. "That was a beauty."

"Well played Sue," said Desmond, who, having been very embarrassed by his partner's behaviour, was anxious to make amends.

The gallery walked forward now towards Desmond's ball further down the fairway. There was a buzz of chatter as people discussed the possible outcome of the hole. Willie and Sue were one down but were near enough the green to get onto it if Willie hit a good shot. That would be three nett two and they might win the hole if Hilary didn't put her shot on the green. Then they would be all square again with three holes to play. But Desmond had hit a very long drive and she could easily reach the green. Her next shot would be crucial, but she was a very good player and if she did get onto the green the pressure would be all on Willie. He'd have to get on the green or they'd probably lose the hole and be two down with three to play. Yes, this shot of Hilary's was certainly an important one which might determine the outcome of the whole match.

Suddenly, as if by magic, all talking stopped. Everyone listened hopefully. Surely Hilary had farted again. Yes, there it was, undoubtedly a fart, a rather disgusting, popping splutter of a fart. The gallery brightened. This was more promising. They drew nearer to Hilary who had stopped to play the second shot. As she took her stance it happened again, louder than before, ending with a most unpleasant wet gurgle. Hilary, gripping the club so tightly that her knuckles were white in contrast to her face which was bright red, made a short jerky swing and managed to hit the ball a full 20 yards. And even though Desmond played a good third shot he was well short of the green. Willie and Sue were also short in three but they had a stroke.

"Isn't this extraordinary William," said Sue. "I feel quite sorry for Hilary. It must be terribly embarrassing. I'd no idea that she had these sort of problems."

"Perhaps she hasn't had them before," said Willie knowingly. "But I'm not sorry for her. Not after that last hole. It serves her right." And, with that remark, he hurried off, anxious to catch Hilary up.

As she walked towards the 15th green, to her horror she produced a musical sequence of staccato farts and, had the gallery listened intently, they would have noticed the close similarity to Beethoven's Fifth Symphony, a particular favourite of Willie's. When she stopped to play her shot Hilary was blushing furiously. She knew there was no point in repeating that she was not responsible for these appalling noises, as it was clear nobody would believe her and she herself had to admit that the sounds seemed to come from her. Perhaps she was farting after all and couldn't feel it. Perhaps she was losing control of her bodily functions. Perhaps she would soon have to wear something. But the possibilities were too dreadful to contemplate and all she wanted to do was get away from everyone. She played a feeble shot which only just reached the green. Willie walked up to her.

"If I were you," he said, "I'd try charcoal biscuits. They make your mouth all black and they taste foul but they're worth a try. After all you've got the ladies' Annual General Meeting coming up soon and you'll want to get your little problem sorted out before then."

And, having dropped that bombshell, Willie turned away towards his ball on the green.

"My God," thought Hilary, "the AGM. All the ladies will be there. Suppose it happens then, in front of everybody, what would I do? It would be awful." She was so distraught that, when it was her turn to putt, she left the ball well short of the hole, leaving Desmond with a tricky putt which he duly missed. Willie and Sue won the hole.

All square with three to play. The gallery was agog. Most of them had expected to be in the clubhouse by now taking tea with the winners. But perhaps Hilary and Desmond weren't going to win after all. Anything could happen now. And what an interesting afternoon it had been. The telephone wires would be red hot after this. It was such a shame that so-and-so hadn't come, she would have enjoyed it. And then there was Marjorie, she'd have to be told – and Jane.

Sue hit a good drive at the 16th, a short par four. Hilary, completely demoralised, teed up her ball and hit it very quickly, anxious to get the shot over before anything happened. The result was a high floating slice. The ball finished in the right-hand rough behind some trees, with 200 yards still to go to the green. This left a good chance for Willie and Sue who were in an ideal position from which to play their second shot. But, as so often happens in golf when all appears to be going well and you have been lulled into thinking a hole is as good as won, fate intervenes and shows who's really in charge of the game.

Desmond took his three wood and aimed for the only gap through the trees. Had it been a monthly medal he would have played out sideways, hoping to get on the green in three and make a bogey five. But he really didn't care any longer. He thought Hilary had behaved abominably at the 14th and just wanted to get the match over. He didn't mind at all if Willie and Sue won; in fact he rather hoped they would. He swung in a carefree, effortless fashion and the ball sped like an arrow, straight through the four-foot gap in the trees, on and up, then finally came to rest on the green three feet from the hole. There was a gasp from the crowd, then a burst of applause. It had been a magnificent shot.

"Shot!" said Hilary with satisfaction.

"Well played," called out Willie with genuine admiration.

"Oh shhh ... ugar," said Sue through clenched teeth.

It was of course inevitable that Willie would top his second and the ball would finish in the greenside bunker. It was inevitable that it finished deep in a heel mark so that Sue had no chance of getting out. In the end Hilary and Desmond were given the hole without even having to putt. Hilary would almost certainly have got the three anyway.

On to the 17th then, Desmond with the honour. A par three with a long sloping green and trouble on both sides, it was the one hole where Willie and Sue did not have a stroke, and Desmond was on a high now. Adrenalin pumping, his competitive fires rekindled, he hit a six iron and the ball finished on the green, about ten paces from the hole. The crowd clapped and then fell silent as Willie teed up his ball. He felt nervous and very disappointed. In spite of all his efforts it looked as if they were going to lose. Somehow he just had to get his ball on the green. He looked across at Sue who smiled encouragingly. She'd played really well. He damn well would get the ball on that green! He took his trusty 3-wood. He swung back slowly, eyes glued to the ball. 'Slow back, slow down, hit into the follow-through.' He could almost hear his father's words to him, spoken over 60 years ago. The ball travelled straight and true, then dropped onto the green about 20 feet from the hole. It would be Hilary to putt first. There was a loud burst of applause.

"Well done William," said Sue, striding purposefully towards the green.

The 18th tee is near the 17th green and, to Willie's profound dismay, Hilary walked to the 18th tee and left her trolley there, taking her putter out of her bag and carrying it to the 17th green. There was nothing he could do. On the 17th at least Hilary was safe. Hilary and Desmond might win the hole and the match here, and he was powerless to stop them.

The crowd had grown now, as word had got round of the great battle in progress. They stood all round the 17th green talking excitedly to each other. This match wasn't over yet. Then there was silence as Hilary prepared to putt. She lined up the putt – straight, uphill. It needed hitting firmly but, even if she missed it, the ball wouldn't run far past the hole. This putt, if it went in, would, she felt, win them the match. But as she crouched over the ball she couldn't help remembering what had happened before when she'd been in a similar position. She hit the ball hurriedly, far too quickly in her anxiety, and missed the hole. However, the ball was quite dead and Willie picked it up and handed it to her.

There was an expectant hush as Sue walked up to her ball. It was not an easy putt, downhill with a borrow from left to right – the sort of putt that should be hit firmly but, if missed, runs on and on giving you a four footer back with a right to left borrow. Nasty. Best to trickle the ball down and make sure of a three. Sue looked up and saw Willie anxiously watching her. She didn't know what had got into him; he so much wanted to win. Normally he didn't take these mixed foursomes seriously but he certainly had today. She'd never seen him like this. Well, she'd somehow get that little ball into that bloody hole! She smiled at Willie and biffed her putt so hard it hit the back of the cup and jumped three inches in the air before dropping back into the hole. There was a gasp of admiration from the crowd, then great applause. Willie, speechless, squeezed her arm and they walked together, heads held high, to the 18th tee. All square with one to play.

"Good thing that went in Sue," said Hilary ungraciously. "It would have been 10 feet past if you'd missed."

"Well done Sue," said Desmond sincerely. "Great putt."

Sue felt quite weak as she stood on the 18th tee, a short par four. Somehow she managed to hit a good drive. So did Hilary. Willie left their second shot just short of the green. Desmond was on it, quite near the hole. Sue putted from off the green but left the ball well short of the hole and Willie did well to leave the next only two feet from the cup. There was loud applause as Desmond quickly picked up their ball before Hilary had a chance to say anything, giving them a nett four. But now Hilary had her putt for the match. It was shorter than the one she'd had on the previous green and nothing untoward had happened on that green. She felt her confidence returning and knew she could hole the putt. It was only what she deserved after all she'd been through. She addressed the ball, totally relaxed now, ready to make one final smooth stroke for the trophy that she so richly deserved.

And then it happened. She cringed as she heard the first sound and could not suppress a cry as she farted again, this time with awesome, volcanic power. A low rumble became a hiccupping put-put-put which developed into a blast of megaton proportions. And then Willie played his trump card. No sooner had the sound died down than those standing around the green experienced the most appalling, disgusting smell. It crept up on them slowly, insidiously, until it was all around. It was choking, revolting, unbelievably dreadful, and the gallery fell back instinctively in a vain effort to escape.

"Shit," said Hilary. "Shit, shit, shit, shit, shit!"

Frustration finally got the better of her. She took a full swing with her putter and hit the ball so hard that it flew over the green and finished in the rhododendrons beyond.

She shook hands quickly without saying a word, pointed her trolley with her clubs in it straight at the rhododendron bushes, switched to full power and let go. Then she hurried to her car and drove away, never again to be seen at the club.

NOT THE SORT OF CHAP WE WANT AS A MEMBER

Willie encounters a formidable adversary.

Act I

Round One

Willie Bradley was happy. As he drove home after spending all morning at the University Dental Hospital he reflected that everything had gone exceedingly well. Beside him, on the passenger seat, lay the golf ball – a new Penfold Ace – a very special Penfold Ace – which, for nearly three hours, had received the undivided attention of one of the finest dental surgeons in the country who also happened to be Willie's good friend.

Using state-of-the-art equipment, Professor Andrew Bailey had drilled a fine hole into the centre of the ball and then, with consummate skill and a sophisticated reaming attachment, had hollowed out a spherical cavity in the centre. A fine syringe was used to inject oil containing magnetic particles into this cavity and the hole in the outer casing was then sealed with resin containing a white pigment.

Professor Bailey picked up the ball and sat back in his chair examining it carefully, then let out a long sigh of relief and satisfaction. It was perfect, indistinguishable from any other new Penfold Ace. He smiled at Willie. Willie smiled back, delighted, and shook his old friend's hand warmly.
"Is it for Edgar?" enquired Andrew.
"It is," replied Willie. "I've to play him next week."
"I hope it works," said Andrew. "Do whatever's necessary to beat that man. He shouldn't be a member of any golf club!"
"I'll do my very best," replied Willie.

Willie decided to stop at his friend George's on the way home and check on progress there. George was in his workshop re-assembling Willie's binoculars, which now had a small but powerful transmitter incorporated that could send out an electromagnetic beam capable of moving the magnetic particles in the golf ball. Without the beam the particles wouldn't affect the flight of the ball, but under the influence of the beam the particles could be moved to one side and alter the direction taken by it. The only problem was that the device needed a lot of power, especially if the ball was in flight and perhaps a hundred yards away. It meant carrying round a car battery on Willie's golf trolley connected to the binoculars. The battery would be fully charged before the round started, but after Willie had used the binoculars George estimated it would take several holes before the battery was recharged sufficiently to be used again. It all depended on the distance travelled by the golf trolley of course.

As Willie watched George putting the finishing touches to the binoculars he couldn't help thinking how much effort was going into beating Edgar. But Edgar was a cheat. A real cheat! A disgraceful, abominable cheat! He wasn't one of the many golfers who regularly carry out minor rule infringements – finding tractor marks or rabbit scrapes on perfect fairways in order to get a better lie, or claiming that the nearest point of relief just happens to give them a clear shot through the trees. No, Edgar, a former RAF officer, was a professional cheat who never lost a ball. Even in the deepest rough he would find his ball when everyone else had given it up for lost and, miraculously, it would be lying quite well giving him an easy shot back to the fairway. Many of Willie's friends were convinced that Edgar was an expert at dropping a golf-ball down his trouser leg. They also pointed out how suspicious it was that Edgar always used golf-balls of the same make and number (Penfold Aces) and made a great show of marking his balls with a red pen, claiming he could always tell them apart. But none of Willie's friends trusted him and many had been beaten by him under very strange circumstances.

The problem was catching him in the act. Even when the unbelievable happened Edgar's opponents never saw the deed actually being done and, although there was much talk in the clubhouse afterwards, nothing could ever be proved. He was the ultimate slippery customer!

Fortunately serious cheating at golf is uncommon, but most golf clubs will, over a period of time, experience it and it is often the most unlikely people who do it – clergymen, school-teachers, those sort of people. Of course the members get to know who these people are, watch them carefully and avoid playing with them if at all possible. Eventually they are caught out and have to leave the club in disgrace to the great relief of the captain and members.

All this went through Willie's mind as he watched George put away his soldering iron. Willie had reached the final of the Veteran's Cup and his opponent was Edgar Batty. The two never saw eye-to-eye on anything and had frequent arguments at the club. They had first crossed swords many years ago in the first round of the President's Putter when Willie was convinced that Edgar had cheated. He probably had, but Willie couldn't prove it. And now they were to meet again, in a final, and the winner would have his name engraved in gold letters on the club's Honours Boards. Willie was absolutely determined that that name should not be Edgar's, for Edgar was, in his opinion, a man without honour, without principles.

As they sat side-by-side in George's workshop sipping glasses of Glenmorangie, Willie mentioned something that had been on his mnd ever since he'd reached the final and knew he had to play Edgar.

"George," he said, "I want you to answer this truthfully and give me your honest opinion. You are one of my oldest and most trusted friends. You know that I have sometimes used unusual methods to win matches when it has been absolutely essential to do so, not always for myself, I might add, sometimes to help others. But do you think – do you honestly think – that this makes me a ... a ... a cheat, like Edgar?"

George said nothing for several minutes before choosing his words very carefully.

"Willie," he said, "there is no way you are like Edgar. I agree that you sometimes use what I call gamesmanship, perhaps even extreme gamesmanship, but it is always for the good of the club or to help a friend. Look how much happier the ladies are now that Hilary's gone and think of old Ramsden, he's like a new man after winning that Old Boy's trophy. No Willie, what you do you do for the good of the club, as you always have, and always will and, if you can somehow sort out Edgar that will be the best thing you've ever done. That man's a disgrace, an absolute shocker, and he's giving the club a very bad name. He mustn't be allowed to get away with anything else. You must do what's necessary to beat him."

Willie felt humbled and very touched by the words of his old friend. It wasn't so much that he wanted to win the cup, he'd won it several times before and his name was already on the Honours Boards. It was that he passionately didn't want Edgar to win and have his name up there with the names of Willie and his friends – all honourable men.

George pointed out that Willie should try the binoculars before his match with Edgar. Why didn't he arrange a game with his nephew Peter and see if Peter spotted anything when they played. It would be an important test as well as giving Willie valuable practice in using the binoculars.

Willie agreed immediately. Peter was his favourite nephew. Willie had given Peter his first putter as a christening present. The little boy had learned to walk with it at an early age and took it everywhere with him. Other children had teddy-bears, Peter had Uncle Willie's putter. When Peter was young Willie spent hours telling him thrilling stories in which golfing 'no-hopers' would win again impossible odds. And Peter was left in no doubt that winning was always better than losing.

The game with Peter was arranged for the following Sunday. It was a warm afternoon and both players played well. Peter had holed two very long putts and was one up with two to play. With the honour at the short 17th, he hit a good shot which finished in the middle of the green only 10 feet from the hole. He was pleased. That should finish off the old boy, he thought. It was time he won; his uncle had beaten him too many times of late and he felt sure he could hole the putt for a birdie.

Willie took his five wood and topped the shot which ran along the path round one bunker and through another, then finished three feet from the hole.
"You jammy so-and-so," said Peter. "That was a terrible shot and look where it's finished! Of all the luck!"
"Time I had a bit of luck for a change," said his uncle as they set off for the green.
Peter looked very carefully from the ball to the hole and decided the putt was dead straight, slightly uphill. Could he make one smooth stroke when it really mattered? He could! The ball ran straight for the centre of the cup

but then, astonishingly, two feet from the hole it abruptly changed direction missing the hole completely.

"I don't believe it," said Peter. "Did you see that! It was extraordinary. I've never seen anything like that before."
And then he stopped, for his uncle was looking at the ball from only ten feet away using a large pair of binoculars.

"What are you doing?" he said. "What's going on?"

"Nothing at all,"said Willie. "What a shame your ball didn't go in. It was such a good putt. Very bad luck!"

"You can say that again," said Peter picking up his ball and looking at it in disgust. And then he noticed that it wasn't his ball at all. It wasn't the ball he'd been playing with for the rest of the round, although he had obviously used it from the 17th tee. It was a Penfold Ace.

After Willie had holed his putt and won the hole, Peter spoke to his uncle.

"You must have given me your ball when you picked both balls up on the 16th green," he said. "You'd better have it back. I don't want it; it won't go straight!"
He thought his uncle looked at him rather strangely as they walked to the 18th tee. They changed balls before driving off.

The 18th is a fairly easy par four which Willie duly won with a four nett three. Afterwards, in the 19th, Peter was still grumbling about his putt at the 17th when he suddenly remembered the binoculars.

"What were you doing with those binoculars?" he asked. "I didn't see you using them before."

"No," said Willie, "there was no need to." He stopped and looked at his nephew thoughtfully.

"Look," he said, "I've something to tell you but I shall need your word of honour that you won't tell another soul. Do you promise?"
Peter looked at his uncle as he stood at the bar sipping a large Grouse. Really he looked remarkably well for a man of 74. His round red face glowed and his eyes twinkled happily behind his old-fashioned round-rimmed spectacles.

"Of course I do," Peter said, to humour the old boy "What's it all about? Don't be so mysterious."

And then Willie told him about the little gadget inside the binoculars and the special golf-ball and the final against Edgar. Peter didn't believe it at first even though he'd just experienced it at first-hand. He didn't think it was possible to alter the direction taken by a golf-ball. But then he remembered being told by his mother that an eminent scientist had once said that Uncle Willie had one of the best brains in the country.

"Well," said Willie, "what do you think about that?" Isn't it marvellous! I wasn't sure it would work but it did, That putt of yours would certainly have gone in if I hadn't steered it off-line."

"Uncle Willie," said Peter, "I am very fond of you. I've always looked up to you but this is ridiculous, beyond the pale! This is cheating! And how you could do such a thing to your own flesh and blood beats me. This is not the action of a true sportsman and past captain of this club."

Peter paused, expecting to see his uncle suitably crestfallen and wilting visibly. Not a bit of it, the old boy was quite unrepentant.

"My dear Peter," said he, "calm down and for heaven's sake keep your voice down. You take everything far too seriously, just like your mother. I'm sorry I had to use the controller against you, but the fact is I had to practise with it. I'm playing that crook Edgar Batty next Sunday in the final of the Veteran's Cup and I must be quite ready by then.

"Uncle Willie," said Peter, "think of the risk involved. Suppose you, a highly respected member of the club were found to be cheating, it would be awful! You'd be asked to resign! Think of the shame and disgrace. Think of Auntie Sue. Don't do it. Those binoculars aren't exactly inconspicuous you know. Edgar will certainly ask what you're doing."

"It won't be as difficult as you think," said Willie. "I've given the whole matter a great deal of thought and I must beat Edgar. That man must not get his name on our Honours Boards. Those boards should only have the names of honourable members on them, not cheats. It's my duty to beat Edgar by any means I can."

"You can beat him properly, Uncle Willie," Peter said. "A golfer with your talent and experience doesn't need to resort to these methods. You can win fair-and-square. I'd back you anytime."

Willie softened visibly. His nephew had hit the right note.

"I'll tell you what," he said, "I'll only use the controller if it's absolutely necessary."

The final was over 18 holes. Peter went along to watch. He couldn't have stayed away! He hoped he'd talked sense into his uncle but wasn't sure. Willie was already at the club when he arrived. He liked to have plenty of time to change and be ready on the first tee at least ten minutes before he was due to start. He had paid one of the juniors to pull his trolley and Peter noticed the large case containing the battery and binoculars fastened to it. It looked very conspicuous, with two wires running from the case connected to what looked like a dynamo on the inside of the trolley wheel.

"Where's Edgar?" asked Willie impatiently. "It's just like him to keep everybody waiting. No consideration. He knows we ought to get off before the afternoon crowd."

"Calm down," Peter said. "Just relax. You're not due off for five minutes yet. Be patient and remember, Uncle Willie, what I said."

Edgar arrived a few minutes later. Obviously enjoying being in the limelight, he made a great show of shaking hands with everyone in sight, much to Willie's annoyance. A number of the more senior members had come along to watch, for it was, after all, an important occasion in the calendar of the Elderly Gentlemen's Golfing Society or *EGGS* as they are affectionately known.

Peter couldn't help thinking what a striking man Edgar was. He was tall and beautifully dressed in smart trousers and a matching Pringle sweater. As Peter looked at him standing next to the rather scruffy figure of his uncle he felt the antagonism that any normal golfer feels when confronted by sartorial elegance and hoped fervently that his aged relative would win.

Of course Edgar's most memorable feature was the black eye patch he always wore over his left ear. No-one knew why. He'd been asked about it many times but would never say. Years ago, soon after he joined, the story had got around that it was the result of his war service. It was rumoured, and never denied by Edgar (indeed there were some who said it was he who had started the rumour), that one day near the end of the war he was limping back to base in his Spitfire, having successfully completed a mission, when he became separated from the rest of his squadron and was attacked by two Messerschmitts. Although badly wounded he fought back valiantly and, against almost impossible odds, managed to shoot down both enemy planes. However the cost to himself was terrible; he'd been hit several times and his left ear was cut clean off by enemy fire. Many said he should have got a medal. Others asked why he hadn't. Edgar never talked about it but would smile bravely and say some things were best forgotten and it was a long time ago. However he was clearly a hero and always acted like one.

One of the juniors claimed to have been present one day in the locker room when Edgar thought he was alone and took the eye patch off. The junior, who claimed to have seen the mangled remains of Edgar's ear, said what a dreadful sight it was and how he'd had nightmares for a week. But of course he was only a junior and not to be believed.

As they walked towards the first tee Willie made his move and Peter's heart sank.

"Edgar," he said, "I realise that in the past we've had our differences. We've often disagreed and I must say it's usually been because you were wrong. However I'm prepared to concede that occasionally I may have been at fault – not often, but possibly once or twice. As a peace offering, to show that there are no hard feelings, I'd like you to accept this new Penfold Ace. I've checked with the Pro to make sure it's the ball you usually use and I hope you'll use it today. I'm confident it will go well for you. Good luck! I'm sure we'll have a most enjoyable game!"

Well of course Edgar accepted the ball, shook hands with Willie and said he'd be delighted to use the Penfold Ace. Peter thought what an old schemer his uncle was and didn't believe for a minute that he wasn't going to use the *controller*.

Edgar won the toss but topped his first drive and his ball only just got off the tee. Willie drove well and marched briskly off down the fairway. The match was on in earnest and there was much at stake. There were no strokes, for both players had handicaps of 22. Willie won the first hole fairly but lost the second when Edgar holed a long putt for a bogey. The next four holes were all halved, neither side giving anything away. The match was being played with grim determination on both sides but, whereas Edgar chatted freely to those watching, Willie kept himself to himself, all his attention on the game. Peter felt proud of his uncle, who wasn't doing anything wrong and was playing very well. Clearly he'd taken to heart what his favourite nephew had said.

The seventh hole is a par three, downhill, with a little stream on the left of the fairway which runs on behind the green. It is a testing little hole which has ruined many a good card. Edgar went first and hit what looked to be a bad shot, for the ball went left over the beck, but then began to curve in towards the green as it always did as Edgar's natural slice took effect. In fact he always played the hole that way, relying on his slice to bring the ball back onto the green. He watched it, pleased. The ball was swinging in nicely when, all of a sudden, it changed course and dropped back into the beck. Edgar swore violently, baffled.

"No need for that sort of language Edgar," said Willie smugly.

"Did you see that?" asked Edgar. "That was a perfect shot. I don't believe it!" He looked round in amazement and there was a chorus of "Hard lucks" and "S'traordinaries", and one or two "Well I nevers".

Peter turned round and saw his uncle quickly putting away his binoculars.

"What a shame," Willie said. "I expect it's the wind. You get some funny little gusts around this green. It was such a good shot too. Coming in nicely."

Willie then played a safe half-shot with a five iron. The ball ran on and on, finishing just short of the green. Edgar played another shot, very like the first but this time it swung in too far, finishing in the bunker on the right of the green. He snorted several times in disgust. When they reached the green Willie insisted on clambering down the bank to retrieve Edgar's ball from the stream.

"It's the least I can do," he said, "after your bad luck going in the beck after that good shot."

Willie then chipped safely onto the green and Edgar, who failed to get out of the bunker with his first attempt, conceded the hole.

On the way to the next tee Peter spoke sternly to his uncle,

"That's enough," he said. "That's quite enough. In fact it's too much. You mustn't interfere with his shots again."

"Of course not," said Willie. "I wouldn't dream of it. Stop worrying!"

But there was a calculating look in his eye and Peter knew his pleas had fallen on deaf ears when his uncle told his caddie, a scrawny, under-fed youth, that he'd give him an extra couple of quid if he could run with the trolley to the top of a small hill nearby and back before they reached the next green. Willie was recharging the battery as quickly as possible.

"What the deuce is going on Willie?" asked Edgar as the lad set off at a brisk canter up the hill as soon as they'd both driven.

"Lad's overweight," said Willie, "and not at all fit. Bit of extra exercise'll do him good."

Edgar looked astonished but said nothing more and the match continued, now in grim silence for Edgar was still upset about losing the last hole. However, whether it was his conscience or the pressure of the final is anybody's guess, but whatever it was, Willie's game suddenly deserted him. He topped and shanked and nearly missed the ball altogether on a number of occasions. Fortunately he was putting brilliantly, otherwise he would have been a lot more than two down on the 13th tee.

Our 13th is another short hole across a valley onto a green cut in the opposite bank. There are deep bunkers in front of the green, with rough and trees on either side. Edgar pushed his tee shot into the deep rough on the right. This time Willie played an excellent shot and his ball was quite near the hole. Edgar's ball should have been easy enough to find but the rough was particularly long just there and, although a careful search was made, it looked as if the ball was lost.

"I'm afraid it's lost," said Edgar to Willie's dismay, for he didn't want that ball to be lost. "We'll have to leave it. Let's carry on."

"Nonsense!" said Willie. "We can't leave it. Now lads (to the caddies) £5 for the one who finds Mr Batty's ball."

"£5!" exploded Edgar. "Have you gone mad Willie, the ball isn't worth that!"

"My dear Edgar," said Willie, "that ball was a present from me. It was a gesture of friendship and as such is not to be lost lightly."

At that point Peter must have swallowed a fly or something for he suddenly had a nasty fit of coughing.

Well, after that offer, the two caddies hunted furiously and one of them had the bright idea of rolling around full length in the rough. He reckoned he'd feel the ball under him and sure enough he did. Edgar couldn't play it of course for he'd already given Willie the hole. Willie cleaned the ball carefully on his sponge, then made a great show of handing it over to Edgar, who felt he had to continue using it although he might well have wanted to change it for another.

"It's turning out to be an expensive game," Peter whispered to his uncle.

"It's worth it," Willie hissed back. "That man cannot be allowed to win one of our major trophies. The honour of the club is at stake."

"What about yours?" Peter enquired, but his uncle walked on unabashed.

On the 14th they both hit their drives as well as they possibly could. They were both on the green in two and Edgar's ball lay only seven feet from the hole, although it was a tricky putt – very quick, downhill, with a left-to-right borrow. Willie putted first, finished stone dead and was duly given the next for his par. But now Edgar had his putt to win the hole. Then he would be two up with four to play – a very strong position. It was a crucial putt. He examined it from all sides, had several practice putts then looked again at the line. Finally he was ready. He hit the putt perfectly. It was the correct speed. He had judged the borrow exactly right. It was a beauty! Under pressure, and in the final too! It was the sort of putt that wins matches and is savoured time and time again during those long nights when sleep will not come. The ball rolled straight for the centre of the cup and was within an inch of toppling in when, inexplicably, it turned sharp left, missed the hole completely and seemed to gather speed as it ran on and on, finishing at least five feet away, leaving Edgar with a very difficult putt back.

"Bloody Hell!" he said, amazed. "How did that happen? That putt was going in! That's ridiculous!"

He was so upset that he missed the next putt. Willie won the hole and they were back to all square.

"Very bad luck," said Willie, putting the binoculars away. "I thought you'd holed the first one. It's a very treacherous green and it needs re-laying. I believe the last time it was re-laid you were the greens' chairman Edgar. It's never been any good since," he added rather offensively.

"There's nothing wrong with the bloody green," said Edgar, very annoyed. "I can't have hit the putt on the right line."

But when he tried again, from the very same spot, the ball went straight into the hole. And it did when he had another putt, and another. He couldn't understand it. He shook his head in disbelief and walked to the next tee examining the ball carefully. It looked perfectly all right. He mustn't have hit the first putt properly.

Suddenly he remembered something odd, although it couldn't possibly have had anything to do with his missed putt.

"What were you doing with those binoculars Willie?" he asked suspiciously.

"Spot of bird watching Edgar," said Willie. "Saw a hawk hovering. Then it dived for the kill. Majestic. I do feel one should not take these matches too seriously. There should always be time to appreciate the beauty of the countryside – the flora and fauna, and all the miracles of nature ..." His voice tailed off and he sighed reflectively, as a man does when capable of appreciating the more meaningful aspects of life above the rather squalid business of trying to win golf matches, his mind operating on a higher, more worthy plane.

Edgar snorted. He was not in a mood to reflect on the beauty of nature, or the beauty of anything come to think of it. Beauty is, after all, in the eye of the beholder and all Edgar could see was the 14th green and a big opportunity missed.

All square. Back to where they had started. Four holes to play. What a battle it had become! Edgar was jittery on the greens now and took three putts at the 15th, so Willie won the hole. They halved the 16th in almost total silence. Both were determined to win, both playing as well as they knew how.

But Willie lost the 17th when his tee shot finished in the bunker by the green. Edgar was on the green. Willie had two unsuccessful attempts to get out of the bunker, then had the most tremendous swipe at his ball, which flew as if jet-propelled out of the bunker, finishing halfway down the ninth fairway. It was hard luck on his caddie who had to run off with the trolley to retrieve the ball. If he'd had any sense he would have left the trolley behind but some of these young lads just don't think.

Suddenly Peter realised what was going on. Willie was trying to charge up his battery. Even a half-charged battery would enable him to alter the line of a putt.

"Uncle Willie," he whispered, "the match is all square. Why not play this last hole fairly? You can beat him. You don't need the *controller*. Please!"

Willie looked at Peter, patted his arm but said nothing as they all walked to the 18th tee. All square, one hole to go.

As he stood on the last tee Peter looked at both players. They had given their all. They were drained. His uncle's usually red face was pale and drawn, and Edgar's eye patch jerked convulsively as the muscles on the left side of his face twitched involuntarily. Peter thought that the last time he'd seen tension like this was on the TV at Kiawah Island when the 1991 Ryder Cup came to a sorry end.

Willie drove first. He hit a bad shot, the ball travelling only about a hundred yards and finishing in light rough to the right of the fairway. Edgar hit a beauty, straight down the middle. Willie played a three wood for his second, hitting a fine shot just to the right of the green but with a bunker between his ball and the pin. Edgar pulled his second into thick rough to the left of the green. They had to search for his ball for quite a long time before Edgar himself found it lying remarkably well in the long grass. It was surprising that it hadn't been seen before. Edgar chipped up to within five feet of the hole. The situation was now desperate for Willie. His ball had stopped on a bare patch sloping down into the bunker, and the hole was just over it. He took out a sand wedge, an old and trusty friend with a razor-like edge and a huge round face. Then he played the most delicate shot imaginable. The ball pitched over the bunker and skidded to a halt within an inch of the hole. It was a beauty. Perfect. Peter felt proud of him. What a shot – and just when needed! He was given the next.

Edgar was down on his knees now, lining up his putt, and Peter wondered if he was thinking of that other critical putt he'd missed on the 14th. Then, as Peter himself remembered what had happened, he swung round and was scandalised to see his uncle getting out the binoculars. Peter hurried over to him.

"Uncle Willie," he hissed, "if you use those things once more I'll report you to the committee."

But it was no use, Willie was already focusing on Edgar's ball. Edgar made a smooth unhurried stroke; the ball ran straight and true, and dropped into the hole! The hole had been halved. The match was a tie. They would have to play again. Peter turned round to his uncle, pleased that, in the final hour, he had resisted the temptation to interfere with the putt. But Willie was still staring through the binoculars, obviously amazed that Edgar's putt had gone in. He put down the binoculars and walked quickly forward to pick Edgar's ball out of the hole. He had a good look at it, went very red in the face, shook hands without saying a word and smiled unseeingly at the many people who came up to congratulate him.

"What's up?" Peter asked. "You look as if you've just had a bad shock."

"I have," said Willie. "Do you know what that old cheat did? He dropped another ball in the rough. He mustn't have been able to find the ball I gave him. I know he drove off with it because I had a good look at it on the tee, but he didn't hole out with my ball. It's the same number and make and everything but it's not the one I gave him. I can tell. They've all got a small mark on them."

They walked in silence down to the Pro's shop.

"Do you know Peter," said Willie, "that man shouldn't be a member of this club. It's disgraceful. But I'll fix him in the play-off. Somehow I must. You do see that don't you?"

He walked away slowly, thoughtfully; saddened by this deplorable lack of integrity in a fellow member.

Act II

A Little Help from Friends

When most of those who'd watched the final had gone home Willie and Peter sat alone at the table in the window of the bar lounge. Neither spoke. The sun was setting now and long shadows stretched across the putting green where the assistant, watched admiringly by two juniors, was mechanically holing putt after putt with the total commitment of one delaying as long as possible the tedious business of cleaning the members' clubs. At the far end a blackbird stood motionless, intent on inflicting grievous bodily harm on an unsuspecting worm. Beyond, the course stretched as far as the eye could see, fairways winding neatly through avenues of trees, greens criss-crossed in carefully mown stripes and the distant hillside resplendent in its autumn colours. It was a time of peace and tranquillity when your average Englishman must guard stoutly against the temptation to do good deeds and give generously to charity.

But there was absolutely no risk of that happening in the bar lounge. Willie fumed. He was furious. He seethed. The knuckles were white on the hand that gripped the gin and tonic. After a while he spoke,

"What gets me," he said quietly but with great feeling. "What really irritates me is that Edgar Batty is an out-and-out cheat and I can't do anything about it. Not a thing! If I complain to the committee they'll want to know how I knew he'd dropped another ball and of course I can't tell them. It's maddening! Infuriating!"

"No," Peter said, "you can't, because you cheated as well. Hoist with your own petard! It's poetic justice. You're just as bad as he is!"

"I'm not!" said Willie indignantly. "That was quite different. Surely you can see that. I'll admit I may have influenced things a bit but I didn't drop another ball in the rough. That's disgraceful! I'd never do that."

"Well I think honours are about even," Peter said. "Anyway, when are you playing him again? You must try to beat him fair and square next time."

"Two weeks," said my uncle, "and I must beat him. I really must. You do see that, don't you Peter? I must win. The name of Edgar Batty must not go on the Honours Boards of this club."

Peter looked at his uncle. Willie's face was very red. His blood pressure must have reached heights hitherto unattained. Peter felt sorry for the old boy. He wanted to win so desperately and he wasn't just an uncle, he was a friend.

"Look," he said, "let's approach it from another angle. Start thinking for a change instead of feeling so annoyed. What do we know about Edgar? What secrets can we unearth from his murky past? How can we nobble him? Legitimately that is," he added hurriedly, for he didn't want his uncle thinking up another of his dreadful schemes.

"Do you mean straightforward gamesmanship, good honest classical gamesmanship?" asked Willie, rather hesitantly.

"Why not?" Peter said. "That's not really cheating. It goes on all the time as you very well know. Edgar's always trying it. He has a reputation for it. Give him some of his own medicine for a change. Do him good!"

"But would it work?" enquired Willie. "He's such an old hand at it. It'd take a lot to put him off."

"Don't be so sure," Peter replied, "and don't be such a defeatist. Start thinking positively like I said. You're supposed to be good at it. Find out what his weak spots are. What worries him? Does he have any problems of a personal, perhaps even of a private, nature? Something he wouldn't want anybody to know about. What upsets him?"

Peter stopped, horrified. What was he saying! Was this really him encouraging his uncle to adopt tactics such as these? He felt ashamed. He was about to tell his uncle he didn't know what had come over him and that he should forget everything Peter had said, but he didn't get the chance. The old boy was smiling. He looked much happier now, far more relaxed, jovial even.

"Well done Peter," he said. "Do you know there are times when you remind me of myself in my younger days. I'm proud of you. It's nice to know that all my efforts on your behalf have not been wasted and the training I've given you is bearing fruit at last."

He leaned forward and patted Peter's shoulder several times before motioning Geoff the barman to replenish their glasses.

"We need information," he went on. "Then we can plan our course of action. I'll have to consult the Three Wise Men and I'll see what Sue can find out too. And you see if that lad of yours can find out anything from the juniors; they don't miss much. I'll tell you what, give young Ben this £5 note; if I know the young rascal that'll spur him into action, and tell him if he discovers anything really interesting there'll be the same again."

He stood up and began pacing backwards and forwards, planning, plotting, scheming. He looked so alert now, so animated, totally transformed from the tired old man of a few minutes ago, restored to his former self. Peter smiled, not for a minute suspecting that his remarks had initiated a sequence of events which, once started, would gather momentum and ultimately destroy Edgar, the former war hero, as Hitler had been quite unable to do. But then Hitler didn't have his uncle's brains.

It is possible that some who do not play golf may be surprised at the lengths to which those who participate in this ancient and honourable game will go in the quest for victory. Some might ask, 'Is it worth it?' Others may question whether it wouldn't be easier simply to practise and improve, thereby making all the chicanery unnecessary. And these people have a point. But it would be much less fun and, anyway, most elderly golfers have long since realised that improvements are things of the past and that all that's left now is a bit of low cunning and guile, and being one step ahead of the opponent who is doing his damnedest to outsmart you anyway. Peter once read an article written by Pat Ward-Thomas about Ben Hogan after that worthy gentleman had won the Open at Carnoustie in 1953, the first and only time he entered. Ward-Thomas described Hogan as an exceptional person with qualities that had made other men millionaires, dictators or destroyers. In Hogan's presence one was aware of a cold killing force, generated from within. According to Ward-Thomas, Hogan bent destiny to his will to a greater extent than any other golfer. Ward-Thomas had obviously not met Willie.

They left the club rather later than intended, Willie smiling, happy at the prospect of pitting his wits against his formidable opponent (and war hero), cheered by the planning and plotting already in hand. They agreed to meet again in a week's time to discuss progress.

When Peter arrived home his wife told him that their son Ben was in his bedroom working hard on his homework and, as he had an important test at school in the morning, he'd asked not to be disturbed. Peter wasn't surprised, therefore, when he went upstairs and found Ben chipping golf-balls over his bed into the wastepaper-basket. Peter spoke severely to him for he did not have his hands far enough forward and was attempting to scoop up the balls rather than hitting them firmly with a crisp descending blow. Peter showed him what was required and he soon got the hang of it; in fact his enthusiasm rather got the better of him and one ball smashed a small pane of glass in his window. Peter promised to get it repaired in the morning. Then they sat on the bed and Ben listened intently whilst his father outlined Willie's request. Ben pocketed the £5 thoughtfully and, when Peter went downstairs, was putting his books away, clearly intending to give the problem his immediate attention. He came into the lounge a few minutes later looking suitably wan, informing his mother that he had a headache and thought perhaps he'd been working too hard. It was only natural for her to suggest a spot of fresh air and perhaps a walk to see his friend for a bit of relaxation. Ben was at first reluctant to go, explaining that he still had a lot of work to do, but eventually his mother persuaded him that she knew best and off he went.

Willie drove home thoughtfully. On the way he stopped at the garden centre and bought a large bunch of freesias. When he got home his wife was nowhere to be found and, although he called out 'Sue' several times, there was no reply. Suddenly however there was a loud crash in the back garden and he saw that a large branch had fallen from one of the trees. On closer inspection he saw Sue. Holding a large saw she was perched rather precariously halfway up the tree looking hot and rather dishevelled.

"Do be careful dear," said Willie. "You shouldn't be doing that."

"Somebody has to!" replied Sue, rather tartly he thought.

"You know I'd like to help," said Willie, "but sawing and then carrying those heavy branches away is very bad for my golf – and my back," he added hurriedly. "It doesn't seem to affect you though; you're very lucky."

"Perhaps it's because I do more," said his wife, clambering down the tree. "Well, how did you get on William? Have you won?"

"All square," said Willie. "We've to play again in a fortnight. But do you know, Sue, that man's a crook. He cheated!"

And then Willie told Sue the full story of how Edgar had dropped another ball down his trousers to replace the one lost in the rough at the last hole.

"But are you quite sure William?" enquired Sue. "I think you must be mistaken. Edgar wouldn't do a thing like that."

"He did," said Willie. "I'm quite sure of it. There's no doubt whatsoever."

"Well, if you're right it's disgraceful," said Sue. "He shouldn't be a member! His wife's such a sweetie too," she added. "She'd never do anything like that. You'll have to make sure you beat him in the play-off. I take it you've had a meal at the club?" she enquired hopefully.

"Well no," said her husband. "I was so upset I just wanted to come home and tell you all about it. I knew you'd understand. I've brought you these freesias," he added, producing the large bunch from behind his back.

"Oh William that is kind," she said. "I do like freesias. They smell gorgeous. Well, if you just wait whilst I saw down a couple more branches I'll make something for you. What would you like – a couple of poached eggs on toast?"

"Anything dear," said Willie. "I don't want to put you to any trouble. I had wondered if we'd any of that fillet steak left and perhaps a few chips and onion rings. But don't worry about me, anything'll do."

Some time later, after they'd eaten a couple of delicious steaks and were both drinking coffee in front of a blazing log fire, Willie told Sue how much he wanted to beat Edgar in the play-off and asked if she'd do a bit of detective work for him amongst the ladies. He was interested in any bits of gossip about Edgar – anything at all, even if it didn't seem important. Reluctantly Sue agreed. She didn't like the idea but she didn't like cheats either and, from what William had said, it did seem as if Edgar had cheated.

The following Tuesday, after the ladies' competition, she casually brought Edgar's name into the conversation and, before she'd finished speaking, someone chipped in with a story about him, then someone else told another, and so it went on. But she didn't feel she'd found out anything useful; all she knew was that Edgar was a very vain man and also one of the world's worst hypochondriacs. Apparently he had a house full of medical books and liked nothing better than to browse along the shelves in the local chemist's shop. He also visited his doctor at least once a month for a check-up.

"That's very interesting dear," said Willie. "So he's a health fanatic is he? Well, well. Did you manage to find out why he wears that black eye patch over his ear?"

"No dear," said Sue, "nobody knows and no-one's ever seen him without it. I don't know about his wife of course; I expect she has but she wasn't at the club. She doesn't come down much nowadays. I'll tell you something though, William, a lot of the ladies think it makes him very attractive – gives him an air of mystery, you know, and reminds everyone what a hero he was in the war. They were saying they'd heard he'd done some marvellous things. That young show-off Sophie Sanders, who wears those ridiculously short skirts, said she'd love to run her fingers through his hair and under that eye patch, just to feel the remains of his ear. Silly young thing! She's played golf with him a few times too, and him old enough to be her father. Daphne thinks there's something going on but I don't believe it, he's far too old."

"He's not all that old," said Willie indignantly. "He's not quite as old as I am and I'm often chased by attractive young women."

"Yes dear," said Sue, not in the least bit worried.

Willie was intrigued by this information and the more he thought about it the more he felt that the key to success in the replay lay beneath the eye patch. What was the true story? What was the secret of the black patch? It was time to consult the Three Wise Men.

Most days they could be found sitting at their table in the window of the clubhouse. It was the best position, with a beautiful view of the course and near enough to the bar for a raised eyebrow to be noticed by old Geoff the barman, then acted upon immediately. Yet it was far enough away from the bar for the noise and bustle not to be intrusive. Geoff, good servant of the club that he is, always kept one eye on the three and could interpret their smallest gestures with unfailing accuracy. He'd had years of practice. Speech was unnecessary. New members were frequently amazed when Geoff would, apparently for no reason, turn away from those waiting at the bar, pour three large gin and tonics, and one small one, deliver the three large ones to the table in the window then drink the small one himself with obvious enjoyment. No words were spoken, no money changed hands. Sometimes, when a captain or president was troubled about a golf club matter he would approach their table and, after a suitable interval, be invited to sit down. They would then listen to what he had to say and nod solemnly, for they'd heard it all many times before. They would then offer their advice and the captain or president would depart a happier man, for their counsel was wise, they were exceedingly old and knew everything and everybody.

It was to these three that Willie went for information. He was always welcome at their table for, years ago, his father had been one of their number.

"Now then young Willy," said Wilfred Waterhouse, the first (and youngest) Wise Man, "how're you keeping? I hear you've to play that young upstart Batty again. Better beat him next time!"

"Quite," said Willie, "that's what I wanted to talk about but, before I do, can I get you all a drink? I see your glasses are almost empty?"
The Three looked briefly at their almost full glasses and smiled approvingly. Young Willie knew how to behave.

"Kind of you," said Wilfred, nodding almost imperceptibly to Geoff behind the bar. "What can we do to help?"

"I wondered if any of you had been on the Selection Committee when Edgar applied for membership," enquired Willie.

"I was," said the Oldest Wise Man. "I remember it well. I voted against admitting him. Didn't think he was the sort of chap we wanted at all, in spite of all the fuss everybody made about his exploits in the war. But I was overruled." He lapsed into an aggrieved silence.

"That's very interesting Horace," said Willie. "I've always thought you had very good taste. Who proposed him? Can you remember?"

"It was Mortimer Binns," said the Oldest Wise Man. "I'm sure it was for I used to play with him a lot before they moved to Scarborough. Mortimer was very friendly with Edgar's father at the Wool Exchange and old man Batty asked Mortimer to propose his son. Mortimer wasn't too happy about it, as I recall, but what could he do? Puts a chap in a very difficult position that sort of thing."

"Absolutely," said Willie. "Did young Edgar have his black eye patch when you interviewed him?"

"Now there's a funny thing," said the Oldest Wise Man, "I don't remember him wearing it then, but I suppose he must have done. It was after the war. Can you remember Herbert?"

"I wasn't on the Selection Committee then," said the second Wise Man, "but he certainly wore it when he was on the committee in '61 and '62. But if you want to know more why don't you go and see old Mortimer? He still lives in Scarborough. He'd be pleased to see you and he knows all about the Battys. Take him a bottle of gin, he'll like that"

"What a good idea!" exclaimed Willie, "I'll do just that."
Then, after a lengthy discussion on the appalling drop in standards at the club, and another little nod to Geoff behind the bar, he left the three and went to the secretary's office to get Mortimer's address.

"Do you remember our old secretary Mortimer Binns?" Willie asked Sue that evening. "I heard from Wilfred Waterhouse that he still lives in Scarborough but hasn't been too well lately. I thought we might have a run over there – perhaps tomorrow if you've nothing planned. We could have a walk along the cliffs and lunch with your old aunt at Ganton. Forecast's good. What do you think?"

"That would be lovely dear," said Sue. "I'll ring Auntie Bea and tell her we're coming."

And so it was that, on the following afternoon, Willie found his way to No. 37 Cliff View, Scarborough, and presented the former secretary of the Black Hills Golf Club with a large bottle of gin. Mortimer was delighted to see him. Over 90 now, he was rather frail but his memory was excellent and the two reminisced happily over old times and former members of the club, most of whom, alas, had long since departed from this life. After a while Willie mentioned that he was in the final of the Veteran's Cup with Edgar Batty and that the two of them had already done battle once. Willie was amazed at the feeling with which Mortimer told him to be sure to beat 'that bugger' in the play-off.

"You proposed Edgar didn't you Mortimer?" asked Willie. "He must be OK if you did that," he added, fishing hopefully.

There was a long, pregnant silence broken only by the regular slurping made by a gin and tonic as it passes lumps of ice on its way home.

"That man's a fraud!" said Mortimer. "I should never have proposed him. I wouldn't have done so if his father hadn't persuaded me it'd be good for the lad after his war efforts. A hero indeed! I should have known better! There'd been some very funny incidents with young Edgar at his previous club. He'd been accused of cheating once or twice – and then there's that eye patch."

Willie listened in astonishment as the full story was told. What a revelation! He had struck gold. For a moment he felt sorry for Edgar, but only for a moment. What he must do now he would be doing for the club not for himself! Standards must not be allowed to decline. Now what would be the best way to play this, a veritable ace of trumps? It would need a great deal of thought, a very great deal of thought. He was unusually silent on the drive home.

Peter arrived at the club early for the Council of War with his uncle and was sitting at a table in the window of the bar lounge when he came in. Peter could see immediately that Willie was in high good humour. He was smiling and spent some time chatting to almost everyone in the bar. He even had a few words for two new members sitting in the draughty corner by the door.

"My dear Peter," he said, "I see you've got me my usual. Splendid. You're looking very well and how is Helen and that fine lad of yours? Did he find anything out by the way?"

"They're both well," Peter replied, "and yes, as a matter of fact he did, although it doesn't seem to me to be a lot of use. I've told him that if that's the best he can do he ought to give you your £5 back, but he said he wasn't so sure about that, he thought it might be important!"

"Well go on," said Willie, "don't keep me in suspense. If young Ben thinks it's important I bet it is. He's much better at judging these things than you are. He's more like me."

"Well," Peter said, "be that as it may, Ben has found out that Edgar's scared silly of wasps. Absolutely terrified. Apparently there's a wasp's nest in the wall by the 12th tee and Edgar won't go near it. He walks right round the rhododendrons so that he needn't walk past the nest, then plays his tee shot as quickly as possible and almost runs off the tee."

"Does he now," said Willie. "Well, well, well! That is interesting, very interesting indeed! That could be just the information I require."

He stopped talking then and his eyes had the glazed faraway look of one deep in thought. After a few moments he took out his wallet and gave Peter a £5 note.

"Give that to young Ben," he said, "and tell him it's just what I require. No, better make it a tenner! He's given me a splendid idea."
And he pressed a £10 note into Peter's hand.

Then he sat back in his chair, motioned to Geoff to bring another round of drinks and told his nephew about his trip to Scarborough. Peter was pleased to hear the news of the former secretary and absolutely astonished when he heard about Edgar's ear.

"That's extraordinary," he said. "I'm absolutely staggered. I can see it would upset him tremendously if people knew about it. If they actually saw the ear it would be devastating for him. But he'll never take off his eye patch. Nothing on earth will make him do that. There's no way you'll get him to take it off. No way at all."

"Don't be so sure," said Willie. "Just think. Suppose Edgar believed he had a wasp trapped in his ear underneath the eye patch. What would he do? According to your lad he's petrified of wasps. Suppose he was convinced a wasp was buzzing about in there, in his ear. He'd take the patch off then wouldn't he? He wouldn't be able to stop himself."

"Hang on, hang on," Peter said. "Let's be sensible. How would you get a wasp underneath the eye patch? Don't be ridiculous. It's just not possible. There's no way!"

"I didn't say I would actually put a wasp underneath his eye patch," retorted Willie. "I simply pointed out what would happen if Edgar thought he'd got a wasp underneath his eye patch. That's quite different!"

"All right," said Peter, "so how are you going to make him believe he's got a wasp underneath his eye patch? I will be most interested to hear."

"My dear Peter," said his uncle with some exasperation, "I do wish you'd use your brains. All that's necessary is to attach a tiny buzzer no bigger than the head of a drawing pin to Edgar's eye patch. If it were black it wouldn't be noticed. I could make it buzz or whine, or hum perhaps, whatever wasps do when they're angry. Edgar'll think it's the real thing, especially if there've been a lot of wasps buzzing around. He'll be scared witless. He'll panic. He won't be able to get that eye patch off quickly enough. You mark my words!"

Willie smiled, pleased at the thought of creating a spot of panic in the opposition and Peter realised he'd done it again. He'd underestimated his uncle. It was so easy to do and so dangerous. He looked so innocuous you wouldn't believe he could think up such devilish plots.

"Uncle Willie," Peter said, "you are brilliant; scheming, conniving, devious – yes – but brilliant. You're right, he's sure to take off the eye patch, anybody would. But think of the effect it'll have on him, on his reputation, his self-esteem. He'll be destroyed. He'll never live it down. He'll probably leave the club. I would."

"Splendid," said Willie, "that's just what we want. Mortimer Binns would be delighted. I've still got a lot to do though. I'll need help from George and from that friend of yours, the one who's keen on acting. What's he called? – Charlie, Dr Charles Loganberry. Will you give him a ring please and ask him to call me as soon as possible?"

Peter's friend Charlie was a doctor, but of philosophy not medicine, and was an industrial chemist with one of the big companies. Charlie was a bit of an actor and could, when necessary, look very distinguished and put on such a confident air that you'd take him for a top surgeon or a cabinet minister or somebody very important. Peter wondered what his uncle had in mind but all Willie'd say was that people didn't usually play well if they were worried about their health.

The following day Willie went to see his friend George. He'd decided professional help was required and George was undoubtedly the man to give it. George was in his workshop cleaning his teeth. It wasn't that his teeth needed cleaning, as he told Willie rather indistinctly through a mouthful of white froth, he was simply trying out his new idea – a combined toothbrush and toothpaste dispenser. He explained that he'd always felt that having to squeeze toothpaste out of a tube onto a toothbrush was old-fashioned and messy, so why not provide each tooth brusher with his or her own supply of toothpaste kept in the hollow handle of the toothbrush? When you wanted to clean the choppers all you had to do was turn a knob at the end of the handle which would screw a little plunger in and push the right amount of toothpaste up the handle and into the middle of the bristles. This was much more hygienic, less wasteful and just the thing for planes, trains and travelling generally. Willie was impressed. They discussed the relative merits of re-chargeable toothbrushes and cheap throw-away models before Willie finally brought up the more serious business of remote-controlled buzzers.

When Willie told his friend what had happened in the match with Edgar, George was appalled. He said that a man like that shouldn't be a member of a club like the Black Hills. Willie agreed. George also said a man like that shouldn't be a member of any golf club. Willie agreed. George said a man like that should be banned from all golf courses. Willie agreed completely. In fact there was so much agreement that things got a bit heated and George had to pour them both large glasses of Glenmorangie before they tackled the finer points of nobbling Edgar. Willie explained his plan. It all hinged on whether George could provide a small black buzzer about the size of a drawing pin head which would buzz like an angry wasp when Willie beamed in the right signal. Of course if the buzzer vibrated as well that would be even better. If Willie could somehow attach the buzzer to Edgar's eye patch he felt sure he could make Edgar believe he actually had a wasp trapped underneath the patch. Then he'd be sure to take it off, any human being would!

George looked at his friend in admiration. It was a classic! Willie hadn't lost his touch, he was as crafty as ever. Now it was up to him. It was clearly a double dram problem so George poured them both another large whisky before lighting his pipe, leaning back in his favourite armchair and closing his eyes. For a while neither spoke. Then George gave his opinion.

"It'll be difficult," he said, "but not impossible. I shall need to buy a few bits and pieces to make a control box, then borrow some things from a friend of mine at the university. But I think I can do it. It'll cost you though Willie; this sort of equipment doesn't come cheap, but it'll work. I'm sure it'll work. In fact it'll be bloody realistic, but expensive. What do you think Willie? It's up to you. Shall I go ahead?"

"George, my dear fellow," said Willie. "You are a genius. The cost doesn't matter. The honour of the club is at stake." He paused for a moment, deep in contemplation. "You know," he said, "there are some things in life that are beyond price, when cost is of no consequence – one's health, the health of one's nearest and dearest, the love of a good woman and beating that bugger in the play-off! You know that as well as I do."

George smiled. He understood completely. Now it was up to him.

The night before the big match Willie rang Edgar. He waited until after the ten o'clock news because he knew Edgar went to bed then and he felt sure that Edgar would think about their conversation and wonder what was behind it all. And something like that can make all the difference between getting off to sleep straightaway or tossing restlessly for half the night until it starts to get light in the morning. The call was quite brief.

"Edgar," said Willie, "I hope I haven't disturbed you. Thought I'd just ask if you wouldn't mind if Charles Loganberry walks round with me tomorrow."

"Who?" enquired Edgar.

"Loganberry," replied Willie. "Charles Loganberry. You know, Dr Charles Loganberry, the eminent physician and diagnostician. Surely you've heard of him? Close personal friend of mine."

"No," said Edgar, "I don't believe I have. I don't know any Loganberrys.

Why's he walking round with you anyway Willie? I thought that nephew of yours would be pulling your trolley?"

"Oh, Peter will," said Willie, "but Charlie Loganberry will be there to keep an eye on me. I'm surprised you don't know him Edgar, with your great interest in medical matters. He's one of the leading physicians in the country. He once told me he could tell what was wrong with a patient before they even spoke to him – from the way they look, their walk, their hand-shake, their eyes, their fingernails, their breath. He's brilliant! I just thought I'd mention it because, as you know, I had a rather funny do recently in a match against Sydney Sunter and Sue has insisted that I have Charles along to look after me and warn me if he spots any danger signs. Then I can have one of my pills. I hope you don't mind."

"Not at all," replied Edgar, "he sounds like a good man to know. I'd like to meet him."

"I knew you wouldn't mind," said Willie, "and I'll certainly introduce you to him. But I ought to warn you not to worry if he looks at you a bit penetratingly. These clever chaps don't seem as if they can ever switch off. He'll probably know just what's wrong with you two minutes after he's met you. Not that there is anything wrong with you of course," he went on hurriedly.

"Well I hope not," said Edgar. "I've been feeling quite well lately, very well really, but of course at our age one never knows."

"And you've been looking well Edgar," interrupted Willie. "I said as much to Sue the other day. Sue, I said, Edgar's one of the lucky ones. A picture of health. No, don't give it another thought Edgar. Charles couldn't find anything wrong with you if he tried his hardest. Well, you get a good night's sleep. I'm looking forward to our little game tomorrow."

"So am I," replied Edgar thoughtfully. "Good night Willie."

The next morning Willie asked Sue to make some honey sandwiches, some for him, some for Edgar.

"What a nice thought William," said Sue. "I'll certainly do that. I'm glad you're not being silly about Edgar. Do you think you might need a bit of energy halfway round?"

"Yes I do," replied Willie, "and I'd like you to make Edgar's sandwiches with that delicious new honey you bought the other day. I'll have the normal thick stuff."

"But William," said Sue, "that new honey is so thin and runny Edgar would get it everywhere! He'd be all sticky. It would get on his hands and his chin. I know it's nice but it's not suitable for sandwiches!"

"Sue," said Willie, "please do as I ask. I especially want Edgar to have that honey."

"Aah ... I see," said Sue. "Well if that's what you want I'll make the sandwiches, but I think it's very childish trying to get him sticky."

"Thank you dear," said Willie, "that will be splendid. And I thought it would be a rather nice idea if you met us with the sandwiches after we've played the 10th, then you can give Edgar his."

"No," said Sue very firmly, "If you want him to have runny honey sandwiches you give them to him. I'll bring them along but I'm not going to be the one to make him sticky. I don't think it's fair!"

"That's all right," said Willie, "leave it to me. By the way, have you asked Sophie if she'd like to come with you? I'm sure Edgar would be pleased."

"All arranged," replied his wife. "She was very pleased when I invited her. She's obviously fond of Edgar and, from all accounts, he's getting far too keen on her!"

"Don't worry," said Willie. "I wouldn't be at all surprised if she suddenly went right off him. If she knew what an imposter he really is, she would."

"William," said Sue, "what are you up to? What's going on? You've got something planned, I can tell!"

But she got no reply for Willie had already gone to change into his plus-fours for the match.

Act III

Retribution

A small crowd had gathered by the first tee in anticipation of what was generally felt would be a hard fought and very entertaining final. Little did those present know what was in store and, indeed, it was fortunate that they did not, for otherwise several of the more kind-hearted members would not have come. After all, it is not a pleasant sight to see a man stripped of his dignity, to watch as the barriers which we all put up to shield ourselves from the world are pulled down until there is no protection and we are seen for what we really are.

Edgar was immaculate. He wore his autumn outfit of matching browns and greens. Willie shook hands and introduced him to a tall distinguished-looking man also smartly dressed but in this case in a well-fitting dark suit, white shirt and spotted silk tie.

"This is Charles Loganberry," said Willie. "Charles, this is Edgar Batty, my opponent in the final."

"I'm very pleased to meet you Dr. Loganberry," said Edgar. "I believe you are very well known in medical circles."

"Thank you," replied the well-dressed one, "I have had some success with difficult cases." His voice tailed away, although he still held Edgar's hand and appeared to examine it carefully before letting it go so that he could tilt Edgar's face upwards. Edgar was conscious of two very bright blue eyes gazing intently into his before Loganberry gave an embarrassed laugh and turned quickly away.

"I do apologise," he said. "I'm afraid I sometimes forget myself, especially if I notice something interesting. Please forgive me! It's a great pleasure to meet you Mr Batty. I've heard a lot about you."

"What do you mean, 'if there's something interesting," asked Edgar sharply. "Do you mean I'm an interesting case? Have you spotted something wrong?"

"No, no, no, no, no," replied Charlie, "nothing at all. Well, nothing serious. Nothing to worry about. Not today anyway. You just get on with your final and have a good game and enjoy yourself. I feel we should all enjoy ourselves more. What does it say in the good book? – 'Live each day as if it were your last.' We should all try to do more of that."

"What have you noticed for heaven's sake?" asked Edgar, now very agitated. "I want to know! You must tell me!"

"No," said Charlie, "it wouldn't be fair. I don't want to put you off your game. I'm only here to keep an eye on Mr Bradley anyway, but I can see he's in such good shape there's little point in my staying. No, don't you worry, modern surgical techniques are wonderful – absolutely first-rate. These chaps can do a bypass in as little as six hours, five on a good day if there are no complications. And there are some splendid tablets." He shook hands once again with Edgar, patting Edgar's hand for several moments before turning away and disappearing as if by magic into the crowd. He was not seen again although Edgar looked round for him on several occasions during the match.

Edgar was considerably alarmed. He reflected bitterly on how unfair life was. You think you're well, in fact you feel well, and all the time the gods are laughing at you, lulling you into a false sense of security until Wham! Bang! they throw a triple bypass at you – or perhaps a quadruple, or quintuple. Now he thought about it he had noticed a bit of pain in his chest and arms lately, in fact it was coming on now and he was feeling very hot. Beads of perspiration broke out on his forehead.

"Are you ready Edgar?" called out Willie. "We ought to get started." He took a coin out of his pocket. "Will you call?"

"Heads," said Edgar. It was tails. Typical, thought Edgar. Well, he might as well play. It might be his last game of golf. And if he had a heart attack and died, well so be it. He remembered Fred Robinson, who'd died in the bunker by the second green during a president's Prize Day and play had been held up for at least half-an-hour whilst his body was removed and the bunker raked. Edgar sighed. He'd play. He'd try to swing very slowly and not hit the ball hard, then tomorrow – if there was a tomorrow – he'd go and see his GP. The old fool should have spotted that something was wrong at his last check-up. You couldn't depend on anybody these days. He sighed again, then swung slowly and sweetly, hitting his first drive further than he'd done for years.

Peter looked at his uncle. His uncle looked at him. They watched as Edgar asked his caddie to pick up the tee peg, then walked slowly up the fairway.

They watched as Edgar, swinging smoothly and without pressing, hit shot after shot with effortless precision. They watched as Edgar holed putt after putt with the nonchalant indifference of one whose mind is on other more important matters. He was three up after five holes and, such is the effect of playing well, having to resist the inclination to cheer up.

On the sixth hole he confided in Willie, explaining the situation and requesting him to inform his wife should anything untoward happen. Now it was clear why he was swinging so easily and Willie realised that Plan A had misfired badly – the biter had been bitten! This was the problem of course with non-golfing collaborators. Charlie had been too clever. He should simply have hinted at dreadful diseases but not actually mentioned any, and certainly not a heart job. People always played better when they didn't hit the ball hard. Willie shook his head slightly. He would know better next time. Fortunately there was still Plan B and yes, perhaps something could still be salvaged from Plan A. He had an idea!

Edgar was four up after the seventh and had almost forgotten how ill he was. He was walking more briskly now and actually hurried after Willie as that worthy gentleman scampered up the hill to the eighth green. He was out of breath when he reached the green and had stopped for a moment when Willie rushed over to him.

"You look terrible Edgar," said Willie. "For heaven's sake rest for a minute. There's no hurry. 1 don't want you dying on me, we're too far from the clubhouse! You're a very funny colour. Greyish. Now Peter, look sharp, help Edgar to that little hummock over there. He must sit down. I insist!"

Play was resumed after a little while but the episode had upset Edgar. He had had time to reflect on how ill he was. He lost the next two holes. Even so he was still two up at the turn and won the 10th easily after Willie lost his ball in the leaves which now formed a thick carpet in the semi-rough on the right-hand side of the fairway. Such a thing, said Willie bitterly, would never have happened to Edgar!

Sue and Sophie were waiting behind the 10th green. Edgar was pleased to see Sophie and the two of them talked earnestly together for several minutes. Sue, meanwhile, was handing round some honey sandwiches. Willie gave some to Edgar, mentioning they would do him good and give him some much needed energy. Edgar didn't really want any sandwiches but couldn't refuse the kind offer, although he soon wished he had when the honey, which seemed of a particularly runny variety, dripped onto his chin, his pullover and all over his fingers.

"Come here a minute Edgar," said Willie, "you've got some honey on your cheek and a little bit on that eye patch over your left ear. I'll just wipe it off."

He took out his handkerchief and, whilst rubbing vigorously at the imaginary bit of honey on Edgar's cheek, managed to place a tiny black disc on the eye patch. George had put a thin layer of adhesive on one side of the disc. Willie also daubed a little of the honey on the eye patch and dabbed a bit on Edgar for good measure.

Edgar was finding it very difficult to get rid of the stickiness from his hands. He wiped them repeatedly on the grass and then on his handkerchief. The blasted honey seemed to have got everywhere! He was irritated and hit a very bad shot at the short 11th which finished in the middle of a large rhododendron bush well to the left of the green.

"You'd better play another Edgar," said Willie, "you haven't a hope of finding your ball in that bush, it's very thick. I hit one in there the other day and found it was so overgrown there was no chance of seeing it."

"Oh I don't know, this lad of mine's got very sharp eyes, he can usually find my balls. Can't you young man?" said Edgar, looking hard at his caddie. Peter looked at his uncle. His uncle looked at him. Then Willie played a shot which finished in the bunker on the right of the green.

"Peter," whispered Willie, "you go with Edgar and his caddie, and don't take your eyes off them for a minute. If he can't find that ball – and I'm damn sure he won't be able to for it's right in the middle of that bush – he'll have to come back and play another off the tee. Even if he does find it, which he won't, he'll have to deem it unplayable, then go back behind the bush and drop his ball in that thick rough. He couldn't drop it at the side because that would be more than two club lengths from where the ball was found. So he'll still have to play over the bush to get on the green even if he does find it, and from thick rough too! He'll never make it, but he's got something in mind, I'm sure of it. You go and watch him like a hawk, he's such a cunning old devil!"

Peter had to hurry to catch up with Edgar. He and his caddie were walking quickly towards the bush. Edgar was not dawdling now. Peter saw Edgar

lean towards his caddie and tell him something very quickly. The caddie nodded. Peter saw what looked like a £10 note change hands. He was still a couple of paces behind them when they reached the bush and, to his surprise, the caddie kept on walking, then dived headlong into the bush near one end and almost immediately called out,

"It's here. I've found it!" And a few minutes later he emerged scratched and grimy, but grinning broadly and holding up a ball for all to see.

"Well done lad," said Edgar, smiling.

"That can't be yours Edgar," Peter said. "Your ball went right into the middle of the bush nowhere near this end. That's certainly not yours."

"Well it's a Penfold Ace and I was playing with that make as you very well know," said Edgar. "But if you don't think it's mine see if you can find another ball where you think mine went in. But you won't be able to, I can tell you that now. This is mine."

So Peter went to look. He did his very best to push his way into the bush at the very spot where he'd seen Edgar's ball go in but it was no use, the bush was impenetrable and there were brambles everywhere. Peter scratched one hand badly. He couldn't even see the ground, the branches were so densely packed. The old cheat had got away with it. His caddie must have had another Penfold Ace ready in his hand when he dived into the bush but of course it couldn't be proved.

"Are you happy now?" enquired Edgar. "I'm sure this is my ball. It must have hit a branch and bounced back towards this end. I believe I'm entitled to a drop within two club lengths no nearer the hole under penalty of one stroke." And so saying he measured off the two club lengths and dropped his ball on a beautiful lush green patch of fairway at the side of the rhododendrons, leaving himself an easy chip to the green. He duly hit his ball to within three feet of the hole and sank the putt for a half in four with Willie.

When Peter explained what had happened to his uncle, Willie shook his head. For a moment he said nothing but gazed unseeingly into the distance. Peter saw a cold bleakness in his eyes and knew then that Edgar's membership would soon be over. He had cooked his own goose. He would now be subjected to a series of events calculated to destroy his credibility and make it impossible for him to remain a member of the club. When Willie spoke his tone was more sorrowful than angry.

"He has run true to form," he said, "and now we too must take the steps necessary to rid the club of this cheat. Plan B must come into operation. You must hurry on to the 12th tee and poke at the wasps' nest with a stick to get the little buggers angry. When Edgar gets there I'd like to have as many as possible buzzing around him."

Edgar approached the 12th tee very cautiously. When he finally arrived there was a large cloud of wasps buzzing all around the tee, particularly in the area of the teeing-off marker. Possibly the tiny piece of bread liberally coated with sweet-smelling honey which had been placed by the marker had something to do with it

"I hate these bloody wasps!" said Edgar, now hurrying to play his shot as quickly as possible. He teed up his ball, straightened up and was just about to swing back when ...

"Stop!" shouted Willie. "Keep quite still Edgar, there's a wasp on your eye patch. Don't move a muscle. I'll flick it off with my handkerchief."

Edgar froze. Panic gripped him. He could imagine the wasp there on his eye patch. Any moment he would feel the sharp stab of pain as the sting went in.

"Oh my God," he squeaked, "hurry up Willie and get the damn thing off me!" And then he heard it buzzing. It sounded as if it was actually on his ear, almost in it in fact. He felt Willie's handkerchief flick at his ear and, to his immense relief, the buzzing stopped.

"Oh thank you Willie," he said, "thank you very much indeed". He was trembling so much that he only just managed to hit the ball, which nose-dived into the ditch in front of the tee. He hardly noticed, he was so anxious to move off the tee.

Willie hit a good drive and, after Edgar had picked out of the ditch, his third shot was still behind Willie's drive. As Edgar was addressing his ball, to his horror he heard the high-pitched whine of an angry wasp, coming closer, ever closer, getting louder all the time. Distracted, he topped his shot, moving his ball less than 20 yards towards the green. Willie played a magnificent shot onto the green and Edgar picked his ball up, conceding the hole.

"You still have a few wasps buzzing around you Edgar," said Willie on the 13th tee. "It must be your sweet personality!"

"I wish they'd go away," replied Edgar with great feeling. "They're a bloody nuisance! I hate the things."

"I can't see any," said Sue, inspecting Edgar carefully.

"Neither can I," said Sophie, waving a small perfumed handkerchief around Edgar's head.

"Take that damned thing away," shouted Edgar. "That smell'll attract more of the buggers!"

"Really Edgar," said Sophie, "there's no need for that kind of language. I'm only trying to help."

But whilst Edgar was waiting for Willie to play first on the short 13th, and wondering what on earth he was doing taking so long fiddling about inside his bag, he heard again the awful sound of an angry wasp approaching, then happily dying away as the wasp moved off. He hoped fervently that it would stay away. His palms were wet with perspiration and he could hardly grip his club.

Willie's tee shot hit the bank on the right of the green, bounced over the bunker and finished close to the hole. There was a polite ripple of applause from the small gallery. Willie smiled, pleased. He bent down, looking for something in his bag as Edgar teed up his ball. Edgar was two up but aware that his lead had slipped. In addition he had a strange and disquieting feeling that events were slipping away out of his control. He couldn't understand it. He must not lose this hole. He must get on the green. He tried to relax and think positively and, as he swung smoothly back he was relaxed, very much so, until he reached the top of his backswing and heard the dreadful buzz of a wasp. It was so loud it sounded as if it were actually in his left ear, trapped beneath the eye patch. The shock was so great he missed the ball completely. A fresh air shot! The gallery was amazed. Edgar could hear comments such as, "Must have lost his bottle." "Pressure's got to him." "Never seen him do that before." "Extraordinary!" And when he looked at Sophie she looked quickly away and would not meet his eye.

"Did you see that bloody wasp?" Edgar asked Willie.

"I can't see any wasps," replied Willie. "Can you Peter?"

"No," said Peter, "there aren't any wasps now Edgar, you must have imagined you heard one."

"I didn't!" shouted Edgar. "I tell you a wasp was near my left ear. In fact it sounded as if it were actually under my patch, but it couldn't have been."

"Well there's nothing flying around now," said Willie, walking all round Edgar and peering up at him intently. "But if you think there's a wasp underneath your eye patch take the thing off and we'll make sure there's nothing there."

"I can't do that," replied Edgar. "There couldn't be a wasp inside my patch, it couldn't get underneath, it fits too tightly. Nothing could get underneath, nothing ever has, not even a midge."

"Right," said Willie, "you know best."

Edgar addressed his ball for the second time but was so upset he shanked it, and it flew off into a clump of trees. As he walked towards them he again heard the hum of a wasp, distant now but menacing, and it seemed to be getting louder. It was still there when he reached his ball and, after two attempts to get out of the trees, and much clattering of the ball amongst the branches, he picked it up and hurried to the next tee hoping to leave any wasps far behind. But that was not to be. The buzzing was definitely louder now and, to his horror, he felt his eye patch move slightly. There it was again, a definite twitch! There must be a wasp beneath the patch, actually in his ear-hole. It sounded very angry too; he would feel the sting any minute.

On his way to the 14th tee many thoughts entered Edgar's troubled mind. He knew he ought to take his eye patch off but knew also that, if he did, all would be revealed and that possibility was too awful to contemplate. He was still one up in the match and desperately wanted to beat Willie Bradley and win the Veteran's Cup. He was very competitive, that was his trouble, he knew he shouldn't have pulled that stroke at the 11th in the rhododendron bush but it had been too good an opportunity to miss and impossible to prove anyway. Perhaps the wasp in his ear would go to sleep or something, it didn't seem to be buzzing much at the moment. If only he could just carry on for a little while longer.

Willie hit a good drive down the 14th fairway and watched speculatively as Edgar walked forward to tee up his ball. He was certainly proving a tough nut to crack but that was what you'd expect. However it was time to bring events to a head. He bent down to his golf bag and his hand closed over the maximum power switch on the remote controller.

Edgar was addressing his ball when the buzzing restarted. It rapidly got louder and louder, and was now accompanied by quite violent twitches of the eye patch. The noise would quieten slightly and then come again even louder ... and louder ... and louder. It was unbearable! With an anguished cry Edgar tore off his eye patch and threw it as far away from him as he could, and there was quietness and peace, blessed peace. And then he realised what he'd done. He looked round and saw amazement and disbelief on the faces of those watching. For they saw a perfect ear, a bit pale certainly as any ear would be if it has been covered up for many years, but not injured, not shot away, not deformed in any way.

"But ... but your ear's perfectly normal Edgar," stuttered Sophie. "It's not been damaged by enemy fire at all. Why have you been wearing that ridiculous eye patch over it? Weren't you injured in the war after all?"

Edgar looked round and saw all the people waiting for an answer, then from the back of the crowd a voice said,

"I'll tell you the true story." And a very old man pushed his way to the front.

"Great Heavens," said Willie, "it's Mortimer Binns. He's come all the way from Scarborough. How long has he been here?"

"I don't know," Peter replied, "I haven't seen him before. I think he must have been waiting in the hut by the 14th tee."

"Most of you will not know me," said Mortimer. "I retired to Scarborough over 20 years ago. But I was secretary of this great club for 30 years and it was I who proposed Edgar Batty for membership. But today I felt it was my duty as an honorary member to return and expose Edgar for the fraud that he is, for I was tricked into proposing him and I hear from my friend Willie Bradley that he's tricked and cheated many of you ever since. So when Willie told me that the final was to be replayed I decided that the time had now come. The truth must be told."

The old man paused and rested a while, for his speech-making days were long past and the effort he was making was considerable. No-one spoke, everyone watched Edgar who stood motionless, gazing open-mouthed at the old secretary.

"Edgar Batty never took part in the war," explained Mortimer. "He is a confidence trickster. He fooled his father and he fooled me. His father was a fine man and was driven to an early grave by Edgar's activities. Just before he came to the club Edgar caught an ear infection and his doctor advised him to cover up the ear to keep it warm. The doctor recommended an eye patch and, when he came to the club, he made up the story about his ear being shot away by enemy fire. He was then looked upon as a hero and has worn that eye patch ever since."

The old secretary rested again, this time for longer. When he resumed his voice was but a whisper and those present moved nearer so as not to miss a single word.

"Edgar Batty is a cheat," said the old man. "Soon after he became a member here I found out that he'd been asked to leave another golf club for activities which were not those of a gentleman. I have to tell you Edgar that you are no longer welcome here and I call upon you to do the honourable thing and leave this club forever."

He stopped, exhausted, and there were shouts of "Hear! Hear!". When the clapping died down there was complete silence as all eyes turned to Edgar. The disgraced 'war hero' seemed to shrink visibly, his face as white as his left ear. He opened his mouth to speak but no sound came out. Then he motioned to his caddie and the two of them set off on the long lonely walk back to the clubhouse.

ABOUT THE AUTHOR

John Atkinson lives in Yorkshire and is a former engineer. He has been a keen golfer for many years and is married to a golfer. They have two sons and six grandchildren.